THE
PASSION
TRANSLATION

Letters
FROM
Heaven

BY THE
APOSTLE
PAUL

Translated from Greek and Aramaic Texts

DR. BRIAN SIMMONS

tPt
BIBLE

BroadStreet
PUBLISHING

Letters from Heaven by the Apostle Paul, The Passion Translation®
Translated directly from Greek and Aramaic texts by Dr. Brian Simmons

Published by BroadStreet Publishing Group, LLC
Racine, Wisconsin, USA
BroadStreetPublishing.com

ISBN-13: 978-1-4245-4947-4 (paperback)
ISBN-13: 978-1-4245-4965-8 (e-book)

Cover and interior design by Garborg Design Works, Inc. at garborgdesign.com
Interior typesetting by Katherine Lloyd at theDESKonline.com

Printed in the United States of America

17 18 19 20   10 9 8 7 6 5

Contents

Galatians 5

Ephesians 33

Philippians 59

Colossians 79

1 Timothy 99

2 Timothy 123

About The Passion Translation 139

About the Translator 141

Galatians

HEAVEN'S FREEDOM

Translator's Introduction to Galatians

AT A GLANCE

Author: The apostle Paul

Audience: The church of Galatia

Date: AD 47-48, or early 50s

Type of Literature: A letter

Major Themes: Grace gospel, justification, the law, legalism, freedom and behavior, and Jesus Christ.

Outline:

Letter Opening – 1:1–9
Paul Defends His Ministry and Message – 1:10–2:21
Paul Defends His Theology and Gospel – 3:1–4:31
Paul Applies His Message Practically – 5:1–6:10
Letter Closing – 6:11–18

ABOUT GALATIANS

Heaven's freedom! This "grace gospel" brings heaven's freedom into our lives—freedom to live for God and serve one another, as well as freedom from religious bondage. We can thank God today that Paul's gospel is still being preached and heaven's freedom is available to every believer. We are free to soar even higher than keeping religious laws; we have a grace-righteousness that places us at the right hand of the throne of God, not as servants, but as sons and daughters of the Most High!

When Paul wrote his letter, the grace gospel was under attack. So, too, was his apostolic ministry—it was also debunked by those who wanted to mix grace with the keeping of Jewish law. Paul begins his letter to the Galatians by making it clear that it was not a group of men who commissioned him; instead, he was a "sent one" by the direct commissioning of our Lord Jesus Christ. And the message of grace that he preached was not a secondhand truth that he got from someone else, for he received it through a direct encounter with Jesus. Paul's ministry can be trusted and his gospel can be believed.

Who was this man, Paul? He was born with the name Saul in the city of Tarsus, the once prosperous capital of Cilicia in southern Turkey. Apparently there was a large Jewish colony in that region. Yet Saul was raised in Jerusalem and tutored by the venerated Jewish rabbi Gamaliel.

Before Saul was converted through a divine encounter, he was considered one of the most brilliant Jewish Pharisees of his day. After his conversion to Christ, however, his name became Paul and his ministry began. Reaching the non-Jewish nations with the glorious gospel of Christ was Paul's passion and pursuit. We can thank God that this brilliant man has left us his inspired letters to the churches.

PURPOSE

What a wonderful purpose is found in this letter from heaven! Shortly after the Holy Spirit was poured out upon Jewish believers in Yeshua

(Jesus), the gospel spread to other ethnicities as well. By the apostolic mandate given to Jesus' disciples, they were sent into every nation. The first converts among the non-Jewish people needed clarity as to the "Jewishness" of the gospel. Was the gospel revelation to be based upon grace or upon keeping the law of Moses? Galatians was written by the apostle Paul to put those questions to rest.

AUTHOR AND AUDIENCE

The chronological order of the books of the New Testament is somewhat certain. However, the first book Paul wrote is often debated; some say it was 1 Thessalonians and others claim it was Galatians. It is my conclusion that Galatians was the first book he penned, possibly around AD 47–48, in order to passionately defend the gospel of grace from those who would confuse and twist the truth. The apostolic burden is always for purity, both in doctrine and in practice, which is why he confronted those who were distorting the gospel of Christ and reminded the Galatian church of the true message of grace.

MAJOR THEMES

Grace gospel. When Paul wrote his letter proclaiming heaven's freedom, there were people perverting his original message of rescue from sin and death by grace through faith in Christ alone. These Judaizers, as they were called, added religious works to Paul's gospel, which placed non-Jewish believers under the thumb of religious bondage to Jewish laws. Thanks to Paul, we are reminded that a Christ-plus-something-gospel is no gospel at all; it is Christ-plus-nothing all the way!

Justification. One of the central issues for Paul in Galatians—and throughout his "Letters from Heaven"—is the issue of how people become right with God and find a "not guilty" verdict for their rebellion against him. The Reformation leader Martin Luther said that justification by grace through faith was the belief by which the church stands or falls. He's right! And Paul explains how it's possible a person can stand before a holy God without being condemned.

The law and legalism. The message of Galatians is clear: Christ's redemptive work on the cross prevents Jews and non-Jews alike from trying to become right with God through religious works; rescue and re-creation come on the basis of faith in Jesus alone. Through his grace, we are freed from the religious bondage that comes from laws and rituals.

Freedom and behavior. The grace gospel brings heaven's freedom from religious bondage. Yet while Christians are free from the law, we are not free to live as we please. Instead, we are called to use that freedom to produce fruit, the "fruit of the Spirit," as Paul says. And it is through the Spirit of God that we not only find freedom but are also empowered to please God with our behavior.

Jesus Christ. As you might expect in a letter about salvation, Jesus Christ stands at the center of this letter. We see that Jesus is fully divine and should alone be worshiped. His cross also plays a pivotal role in Paul's grace-letter, for it is through his sacrifice alone that believers are made right with God.

———

A great many truths await us as we read and embrace the revelation he shares with us today. May the Lord bring his glory into your heart as you read this God-breathed and heavenly inspired letter to the Galatians! Take it as the gospel truth.

One

___

Dear friends,

[1] My name is Paul[a] and I have been commissioned as an apostle[b] of the Lord Jesus, the Messiah. You need to know that my apostolic authority was not granted to me by any council of men, for I was appointed by Jesus, the Anointed One, and God the Father, who raised him from the dead. [2] I am joined by all the brothers and sisters[c] who are here with me as I write you this letter, which is to be distributed to the churches throughout the region of central Turkey.[d]

[3-4] I pray over you a release of the blessings of God's undeserved kindness and total well-being[e] that flows from our Father-God and from the Lord Jesus.[f] He's the Anointed Messiah who offered his soul as the

a 1:1 The name Paul means "little." His name before his conversion was Saul, which means "significant one" or "sought after." What great transformation takes place when we experience a profound change like Saul did! God transforms us from being "important" to being "small" in our own eyes. This is what qualifies God's apostolic servants.

b 1:1 The word *apostle* means "one who is sent on a mission" or "an ambassador." By implication, an apostle carries the delegated authority of the one who sends him. Paul was chosen by Jesus Christ as an apostle to plant churches and impart the revelation of Christ and his true gospel. There are more references in the New Testament about the gift of apostle than all the other gifts (prophet, evangelist, pastor, and teacher) combined. See Ephesians 4:11.

c 1:2 The Greek word *adelphos* is used throughout the New Testament for brothers (and sisters). It is used in classical Greek by physicians to describe "those who came from the same womb." We are all truly born from the same "womb" of the Father's heart and the wounded side of Jesus Christ. In the time of Alexander the Great, the word *adelphos* was used not only for brothers (and sisters), but for "faithful soldiers." How wonderful it is in our journey to know that we have those fighting for the faith alongside of us who are born from the same womb and faithful partners in our battles.

d 1:2 Or "Galatia." This was the region in Asia Minor (modern day Turkey) that Paul visited during his first and second missionary journeys. See Acts 16:1–5.

e 1:3–4 This is the word *peace*, which in the Hebraic mindset means "health, prosperity, peace, and total well-being."

f 1:3–4 Grace was not just a "message" that Paul taught; it was the way he dealt with deceived people. Even over the confused churches that were mixing works and grace, Paul spoke words of blessing and peace. When we learn to bless and release "undeserved kindness" and

sacrifice[a] for our sins! He has taken us out of this evil world system[b] and set us free through our salvation, just as God desired. [5]All the glory will go to God alone, throughout time and eternity. Amen!

[6]I am shocked over how quickly you have deserted the grace gospel[c] and strayed away from the Anointed One who called you to himself by his loving mercy. I'm frankly astounded that you now embrace a distorted gospel of salvation by works! [7]That is a fake "gospel" that is simply not true. There is only one gospel—the gospel of the Messiah! Yet you have allowed those who mingle law with grace to confuse you with lies.

[8]Anyone who comes to you with a different message than the grace gospel that you have received will have the curse of God come upon them! For even if we or an angel appeared before you, to give you a different gospel than what we have already proclaimed, God's curse will be upon them.

[9]I will make it clear: Anyone, no matter who they are, that brings you a different gospel than the grace gospel that you have received, let them be condemned and cursed!

[10]I'm obviously not trying to flatter you or water down my message to be popular with men, but my supreme passion is to please God. For if all I attempt to do is please people, I would not be the true servant of the Messiah.

[11]Beloved ones, let me say emphatically that the gospel entrusted to me was not given to me by any man. [12]No one taught me this

---

"well-being" over those who oppose us, perhaps then they will listen to us.

a   1:3–4 As translated from the Aramaic text.

b   1:3–4 This "evil world system" would include the religious system that is based on duty and performance instead of love and grace.

c   1:6 Implied by the context of Galatians. The Aramaic text reads simply "the hope."

revelation, for it was given to me directly by the unveiling of Jesus the Anointed One before my eyes.

[13]By now you have heard stories of how severely[a] I harassed and persecuted Christians and did my best to systematically destroy God's church, all because of my radical devotion to preserve the traditions of the Jewish religion. [14]My zeal and passion for the doctrines of Judaism distinguished me among my people, for I was far more advanced in my religious instruction than others my age.

[15]But then something happened! God called me by his grace; and in love, he chose me from my birth to be his. [16]God's grace unveiled his Son in me so that I would proclaim the message of "sonship"[b] to the non-Jewish people of the world. After I had this encounter I kept it a secret for some time, sharing it with no one. [17]And I chose not to run to Jerusalem to try to impress those who had become apostles before me. Instead, I went away into the Arabian Desert for a season until I returned to Damascus, where I had first encountered Jesus.[c] [18]I remained there for three years until I eventually went up to Jerusalem and met the Apostle Peter[d] and stayed with him for a couple of weeks so I could get to know him better. [19]The only other apostle I met during that time was James,[e] the Lord's brother.

[20]Everything I'm describing to you I confess before God is the absolute truth. [21]After my stay in Jerusalem, I went to Syria and southeast Turkey,[f] [22]but remained unknown to the Jewish believers in Judea.

---

a 1:13 The Aramaic is "beyond measure."
b 1:16 Implied by the context of Paul's writings. All of Paul's teachings could be summed up in this concept of revealing the truth of our "sonship" to the nations.
c 1:17 Implicit information added for the sake of English narrative.
d 1:18 The Aramaic name of Peter is *kefa*, which means "rock."
e 1:19 Or "Jacob."
f 1:21 Or "Cilicia," which was the southeastern province of Asia Minor, directly adjoining Syria.

[23]The only thing they heard about me was this: "Our former enemy, who once brutally persecuted us, is now preaching the good news of the faith that he was once obsessed with destroying!" [24]Because of the transformation that took place in my life, they praised God even more![a]

Two

———

[1]Fourteen years later I returned to Jerusalem, this time with Barnabas[b] and Titus,[c] my coworkers.[d] [2]God had given me a clear revelation[e] to go and confer with the other apostles concerning the message of grace I was preaching to the non-Jewish people. I spoke privately with those who were viewed as senior leaders of the church. I wanted to make certain that my labor and ministry for the Messiah had not been based on a false understanding of the gospel.[f]

My hope was that they would agree with my grace message, and indeed, they did agree, affirming the truth of what I had been teaching. [3]They even accepted Titus[g] without demanding that he follow strict

---

a   1:24 The Aramaic text states "they glorified God for having me."

b   2:1 Barnabas is an Aramaic name that means "son of encouragement."

c   2:1 Titus was a Gentile convert to Christ and was a frequent companion of Paul's. Later Paul wrote a beautiful letter to Titus. Titus' name means "nurse."

d   2:1 Implied in the text and supplied for the sake of English narrative.

e   2:2 Although we don't know exactly what the *clear revelation* might have been, it is possible it came in the form of a dream, a vision, a prophecy, or an angel that appeared to Paul.

f   2:2 The Greek text states "running the race for nothing."

g   2:3 Titus was converted through Paul's ministry and was later sent out by Paul as an apostolic church planter. The book of Titus was written by Paul to his spiritual son to give him encouragement and revelation for his ministry.

Jewish customs[a] before they would receive him as a brother[b] since he was a Syrian[c] and not a Jew.

[4]I met with them privately and confidentially because false "brothers" had been secretly smuggled into the church meetings. They were sent to spy on the wonderful liberty and freedom that we have in Jesus the Anointed One, and to see if we were faithfully keeping the Jewish regulations. Their agenda was to bring us back into the legalistic bondage of religion. [5]But you must know that we did not submit to their religious shackles[d] not even for a moment, so that we might keep the gospel of grace unadulterated for you.

[6]Even the most honored and esteemed among the brothers were not able to add anything to my message. Who they are before men makes no difference to me, for God is not impressed by the reputations[e] of men. [7]So they concluded that I was entrusted with taking the gospel to the non-Jewish people just as Peter was entrusted with taking it to the Jews. [8]For the same God who anointed Peter to be an apostle to the Jews also anointed me as an apostle to those who are not Jewish.

[9]When they all recognized this grace operating in my ministry, James, Peter, and John, the esteemed followers[f] of Jesus, extended to me the warmth of Christian fellowship and honored[g] my calling to minister to the non-Jewish people. [10]They simply requested one thing of

---

a 2:3 Or "be circumcised."

b 2:3 "Receive him as a brother," although not in the text, is implicit within the context.

c 2:3 Or "Aramean," which is an Aramaic-speaking Gentile. Syrians are Arameans, but Greeks are not. Most Greek manuscripts identify Titus as a Greek when, in fact, he was Syrian. It is believed that the Greek copies of the manuscript changed Titus' ethnicity to Greek, but the Aramaic text correctly identifies him as a Syrian.

d 2:5 Or in Aramaic, "their efforts to enslave us" or "their oppression."

e 2:6 Or "masks."

f 2:9 Or "pillars."

g 2:9 Or in Aramaic "they gave me the right to proceed."

me: that I would be devoted to the poor and needy,[a] which was the burden I was already carrying in my heart.

[11]But when Peter visited Antioch,[b] he began to mislead the believers and caused them to stumble over his behavior, so I had to confront him to his face over what he was doing. [12]He enjoyed being with the non-Jewish believers who didn't keep the Jewish customs, eating his meals with them—up until the time the Jewish friends of James arrived from Jerusalem. When he saw them, he withdrew from his non-Jewish friends and separated himself from them, acting like an orthodox Jew—fearing how it would look to them if he ate with the non-Jewish believers.[c]

[13]And so because of Peter's hypocrisy,[d] many other Jewish believers followed suit, forming a clique and refusing to eat with non-Jewish believers. Even Barnabas was led astray by Peter's poor example and condoned this legalistic, hypocritical behavior!

[14]So when I realized they weren't being honest to what they believed and were acting inconsistently with the revelation of grace, I confronted Peter in front of everyone:

"You're born a Jew and yet you've chosen to disregard Jewish regulations and live like a Gentile.[e] Why then do you force those who are not Jews to conform to the regulations of Judaism, just to make a good impression on your Jewish friends?

---

a 2:10 As translated from the Aramaic.
b 2:11 Antioch was a large city in Syria with a significant Jewish population. It was in Antioch that believers were first called Christians and it was the first church to send out missionaries to the nations. See Acts 11:25; 13:1–3.
c 2:12 Or "those who were not of the circumcision."
d 2:13 The incident of Acts 10–11 happened before this account in Galatians 2. Peter was shown by a heavenly vision that God views the non-Jewish believers as "clean." This amplifies Peter's hypocrisy. Even Jesus' apostles had conflicts that needed to be worked out and healed.
e 2:14 Some Aramaic translators translate this word "Syrian" or "Aramean."

¹⁵Although we're Jews by birth and not non-Jewish "sinners," ¹⁶we know full well that we don't receive God's perfect righteousness as a reward for keeping the law, but by the faith of Jesus the Messiah!ᵃ His faithfulness, not ours, has saved us, and we have received God's perfect righteousness. Now we know that God accepts no one by the keeping of religious laws, but by the gift of grace!"ᵇ

¹⁷If we are those who desire to be saved from our sins through our union with the Anointed One, does that mean our Messiah promotes our sins if we still acknowledge that we are sinners? How absurd! ¹⁸For if I start over and reconstruct the old religious system that I have torn down with the message of grace, I will appear to be one who turns his back on the truth.

¹⁹It was when I tried to obey the law that I was condemned with a curse,ᶜ because I'm not able to fulfill every single detail of it. But because the Messiah lives in me, I've now died to the law's dominion over me so that I can live for God.

²⁰My old identity has been co-crucified with Messiah and no longer lives; for the nails of his cross crucified me with him. And now the essence of this new life is no longer mine, for the Anointed One lives his life through me—we live in union as one! My new life is empowered by the faith of the Son of God who loves me so much that he gave himself for me, and dispenses his life into mine!ᵈ

²¹So that is why I don't view God's grace as something minor or

---

a 2:16 The Aramaic and Greek is clearly "the faith of Jesus, the Messiah." It is not simply our faith, but his—the faithfulness of Jesus to fulfill the Father's pleasure in his life and the sacrifice for our sins in his death. Salvation is found in the "faith of Jesus."

b 2:16 Implied by the context.

c 2:19 Although implicit here, the mention of the "curse" can be found in Galatians 3:10.

d 2:20 The last sentence of this verse in Aramaic is plural, "us."

peripheral. For if keeping the law could release God's righteousness to us, the Anointed One would have died for nothing."

Three
___

[1]What has happened to you Galatians to be acting so foolishly? You must have been under some evil spell[a] to have missed the revelation of truth! Didn't God open your eyes to see the meaning of Jesus' crucifixion? Wasn't he revealed to you as the Manifestation of Wisdom?[b]

[2]So answer me this: Did the Holy Spirit come to you as a reward for keeping all the Jewish laws? No, you received him as a gift because you believed in the Messiah. [3]Your new life in the Anointed One began with the Holy Spirit giving you a new birth. Why then would you so foolishly turn from living in the Spirit to becoming slaves again to your flesh?[c] Do you really think you can bring yourself to maturity in the Anointed One without the Holy Spirit?[d]

[4]Have you endured all these trials and persecutions for nothing?

[5]Let me ask you again: What does the lavish supply of the Holy Spirit in your life, and the miracles of God's tremendous power,[e] have to

---

a   3:1 The Greek word used here means "to cast a spell using the evil eye." Paul uses a pun here in the Greek text. He goes on to say, "Didn't God *open* your eyes?"

b   3:1 This very unusual sentence is translated from the Aramaic text. The words, "Manifestation of Wisdom" can also be translated, "Artisan" or "Fashioner" or "Master Craftsman." This term points us to the uncreated "Wisdom" spoken of in Proverbs 8. Jesus has been crucified for us; this has resulted in his "house," the church, being built. The great revelation of the cross had been supernaturally given to them; but they were diluting the glorious work of the cross by adding to it the works of religion.

c   3:3 As translated from the Aramaic.

d   3:3 Implied in the text.

e   3:5 As translated from the Greek. The Aramaic text states "God's covenant of power."

do with you keeping religious laws? The Holy Spirit is poured out upon us through the revelation and power of faith, not by keeping the law!

[6]Abraham, our father of faith, led the way as our pioneering example. He believed God and the substance of his faith released God's righteousness to him.[a] [7]So those who are the true children of Abraham will have the same faith as their father! [8]God's plan all along was to bring this message of salvation to the nations through the revelation of faith. Long ago God prophesied over Abraham, as the Holy Scriptures say:

"Through your example of faith all the nations will be blessed!"[b]

[9]And so the blessing of Abraham's faith is now our blessing too! [10]But if you choose to live in bondage under the legalistic rule of religion, you live under the law's curse. For it is clearly written:

**"Utterly cursed is everyone who fails to practice
every detail and requirement that is written in this Law!"**[c]

[11]For the Scriptures reveal, and it is obvious, that no one achieves the righteousness of God by attempting to keep the law, for it is written:

"Those who have been made holy will live by faith!"[d]

[12]But keeping the law does not require faith, but self-effort. For the Law teaches,

---

a   3:6 See Genesis 15:6.
b   3:8 See Genesis 12:3; 18:18; 22:18.
c   3:10 See Deuteronomy 27:26.
d   3:11 See Habakkuk 2:4.

> **"If you practice the principles of law,**
> **you must follow all of them."**[a]

[13]Yet, Messiah, our Anointed Substitute, paid the full price to set us free from the curse of the law. He absorbed it completely as he became a "curse" in our place. For it is written:

> **"Everyone who is hung upon a tree is doubly cursed."**[b]

[14]Jesus, our Messiah was hung upon a "tree," bearing the curse in our place and in so doing, dissolved it from our lives, so that all the blessings of Abraham can be poured out upon even non-Jewish believers. And now God shows grace to all of us and gives us the promise of the wonderful Holy Spirit who lives within us when we believe in him.

[15]Beloved friends, let me use an illustration that we can all understand. Technically, when a contract is signed, it can't be changed after it has been put into effect; it's too late to alter the agreement.[c]

[16]Remember the royal proclamation[d] God spoke over Abraham and to Abraham's child? God said that his promises were made to pass on to Abraham's "Child,"[e] not children. And who is this "Child?" It's the Son of promise, Jesus, the anointed Messiah!

[17-18]This means that the covenant between God and Abraham was fulfilled in Messiah and cannot be altered. Yet the written Law was not even given to Moses until 430 years later, after God had "signed"

---

a 3:12 See Leviticus 18:5.
b 3:13 See Deuteronomy 21:23.
c 3:15 The most ancient Aramaic manuscript has a different meaning for this verse. It could also be translated, "The covenant of the Son of Man that I reference should never be denigrated or changed in any way by men."
d 3:16 As translated literally from the Greek. It can also mean "covenant."
e 3:16 Or "seed."

his contract with Abraham! The Law, then, doesn't supersede the promise[a] since the royal proclamation was given before the Law.[b]

Because we are united with the Anointed One, all the promises of the kingdom are deeded to us, not because we keep the Law or fulfill religious duties. If that were the case, it would have nullified what God said to Abraham. We receive all the promises because of the Promised One—not because we keep the Law!

[19]Why then was the Law given? It was an intermediary agreement added after the promise was given to show men how guilty they are! It remained in force until the Joyous Expectation[c] was born to fulfill the promises given to Abraham.

And here's another contrast: When God gave the Law, he didn't give it to them directly, for he gave it first to the angels; they gave it to his mediator,[d] who then gave it to the people. [20]But when God entered into covenant with Abraham, there was no middleman, no go-between—he gave it directly and fulfilled it all by himself!

[21]Since that's true, should we consider the written Law to be contrary to the promise of new life? How absurd![e] Truly, if there was a law that we could keep which would give us new life, then our salvation would have come by law-keeping. [22]But the Scriptures make it clear that since we were all under the power of sin, we needed Jesus! And he is the Savior who brings the kingdom realm[f] to those who believe.

---

a 3:17–18 The concept of the "promise" is that all we need is faith to believe it. This is the revelation of grace that saves us, for the "promise" is enough.

b 3:17–18 This last sentence, although not in the text, is the implied conclusion of Paul's logic.

c 3:19 The "Joyous Expectation" is translated literally from the Aramaic and obviously refers to Jesus Christ.

d 3:19 This would be Moses. However, the ancient Aramaic says, "The one who was able."

e 3:21 The law and the promise (grace) each have a distinct function. The law brings conviction of sin, which unveils grace as the way to salvation. The law moves us, even compels us, to reach for grace. And grace will cause one to soar even higher than the demands of the law.

f 3:22 As translated from the Aramaic.

²³So until the revelation of faith for salvation was released, the Law was a jailor, holding us as prisoners under lock and key until the "faith," which was destined to be revealed, would set us free. ²⁴The Law and our failure to keep it becomes a gateway to lead us to the Messiah so that we would be saved by faith. ²⁵But when faith comes into our hearts, and we have come to the Messiah, the Law is no longer in force, since we have already entered into life.

²⁶You have all become true children of God by the faith of Jesus the Anointed One![a] ²⁷It was faith that immersed you into Jesus, the Anointed One, and now you are covered and clothed with his anointing. ²⁸And we no longer see each other in our former state—Jew or non-Jew, rich or poor,[b] male or female—because we're all one through our union with Jesus Christ with no distinction between us.

²⁹And since you've been united to Jesus the Messiah, you are now Abraham's "child" and inherit all the promises of the kingdom realm!

Four

¹As you know, when children are promised something, they won't forget until they receive it. In a similar way, God has promised our ancestors something better, but as long as an heir is a minor, he's not really much different than a servant, although he's the master over all of them. ²For until the time appointed by the father when he comes of age, the child is under the domestic supervision of the guardians of the estate.

---

a 3:26 It is the "faith of Jesus," or what he believes about you, that makes you his very own.
b 3:28 Implied in the text. The Greek text literally means "enslaved or free."

³So it is with us. When we were juveniles we were enslaved under the regulations and rituals of religion.ᵃ ⁴But when that era came to an end and the time of fulfillment had come, God sent his Son, born of a woman,ᵇ born under the written Law. ⁵Yet all of this was so that he would redeem and set free all those held hostage to the written Law so that we would receive our freedom and a full legal adoption as his children.

⁶And so that we would know for sure that we are his true children, God released the Spirit of Sonship into our hearts—moving us to cry out intimately, "My Father!ᶜ You're our true Father!"

⁷Now we're no longer living like slaves under the law, but we enjoy being God's very own sons and daughters! And because we're his, we can access everything our Father has—for we are one with Jesus the Anointed One!ᵈ

⁸Before we knew God as our Father and we became his children, we were unwitting servants to the powers that be, which are nothing compared to God. ⁹But now that we truly know him and understand how deeply we're loved by him, why would we, even for a moment, consider turning back to those weak and feeble principles of religion, as though we were still subject to them?

¹⁰Why would we want to go backwards into the bondage of religion—scrupulously observing rituals like special days,ᵉ celebrations of

---

a   4:3 As translated from the Aramaic. The Greek text states "We were in bondage to the hostile spirits of the world."

b   4:4 Every child has a mother; but for Jesus to be "born of a woman" meant there was no human father, no male counterpart. Jesus' true Father is the Father of Eternity. No other child has had a virgin birth, "born of a woman," except him. All the rest of us are born from a father and a mother.

c   4:6 This is the Aramaic word *Abba* which means "my father." *Abba* was borrowed by the Greeks and is found in the Greek manuscripts as well.

d   4:7 As translated from the Aramaic.

e   4:10 Or "Sabbaths." There is no requirement for Gentiles to become like Jews and observe the new moon, annual festivals, and sacred years?[a] [11]I'm so alarmed about you that I'm beginning to wonder if my labor in ministry among you was a waste of time!

[12]Beloved ones, I plead with you, follow my example and become free from the bondage of religion. I once became as one of you,[b] a Gentile, when I lived among you—now become free like me. When I first came to minister to you, you did me no wrong. I can't believe you would do wrong to me now!

[13]You are well aware that the reason I stayed among you to preach the good news was because of the poor state of my health.[c] [14]And yet you were so kind to me and did not despise me in my weakness,[d] even though my physical condition put you through an ordeal while I was with you.

Actually, you received me and cared for me as though I were an angel from God, as you would have cared for Jesus, the Messiah himself! [15]Some of you were even willing, if it were possible, to pluck out your own eyes to replace mine! Where is that kindhearted and free spirit now? [16]Have I really become your enemy because I tell you the truth?

[17]Can't you see what these false teachers[e] are doing? They want

---

Jewish ordinances in order to draw closer to God. Our approach to God is always on the basis of grace and faith in the blood of Jesus Christ, the Lord of the Sabbath.

a 4:10 These terms could also apply to following astrological signs.

b 4:12 Or "imitated you." Paul is using sarcasm and saying, "I imitated you; now you should imitate me!"

c 4:13 Paul's ministry in Antioch began when he became sick and had to delay his missionary journey to other regions. He may have been afflicted with an illness that normally aroused disgust by reason of its repulsive nature. Many surmise that Paul contracted an ophthalmic disorder (an eye disease), which was prevalent in the region. The illness can cause one to have a repugnant appearance. Other scholars think he was simply very ill as a result of his treatment by his enemies on his first missionary journey. Still the Galatians did not reject him; instead they welcomed him with open arms, and his gospel message with open hearts.

d 4:14 The Aramaic word can also mean "sickness."

e 4:17 Or "whispering enemies."

to win you over so you will side with them. They want you divided from me so you will follow only them. Would you call that integrity? [18]Isn't it better to seek excellence and integrity always, and not just only when I'm with you?

[19]You are my dear children, but I agonize in spiritual "labor pains" once again, until the Anointed One will be fully formed in your hearts and become visible through your lives! [20]How I wish I could be there in person to clearly convey my thoughts and change my tone[a] toward you, for I am truly dumbfounded over what you are doing!

[21-22]Tell me, do you want to go back to living strictly by the Law? Haven't you ever listened to what the Law really says? Have you forgotten that Abraham had two sons; one by the slave girl, and the other by the freewoman?[b]

[23]Ishmael, the son of the slave girl, was a child of the natural realm. But Isaac, the son of the freewoman, was born supernaturally by the Spirit—a child of the promise of God! [24]These two women and their sons express an allegory and become symbols of two covenants. The first covenant was born on Mt. Sinai, birthing children into slavery—children born to Hagar. [25]For "Hagar" represents the Law given at Mt. Sinai in Arabia. The "Hagar" metaphor corresponds to the earthly Jerusalem of today who are currently in bondage.

[26]In contrast, there is a heavenly Jerusalem above us, which is our true "mother." She is the freewoman, birthing children into freedom![c] [27]For it is written:

"Burst forth with gladness,

---

a   4:20 The Aramaic word is actually "echo."

b   4:22 See Genesis 16:15; 21:2.

c   4:26 Paul is showing that the law is a system of works that brings bondage and that the promise is a system of grace that brings true freedom.

O barren woman with no children!
Break through with the shouts of joy and jubilee,
for you are about to give birth!
The one who was once considered desolate and barren
now has more children than the one who has a husband!"[a]

[28]Dear friends, just like Isaac, we're now the true children who inherit the kingdom promises.[b] [29]And just as the son of the natural world at that time harassed the son born of the power of the Holy Spirit, so it is today. [30]And what does the Scripture tell us to do?

"Expel the slave mother with her son![c]
The son of the slave woman will not be a true heir—
for the true heir of the promises is the son of the freewoman." [d]

[31]It's now so obvious! We're not the children of the slave woman; we're the supernatural sons of the freewoman—sons of grace!

Five

[1]Let me be clear, the Anointed One has set us free—not partially, but completely and wonderfully free! We must always cherish this truth and stubbornly refuse to go back into the bondage of our past.

[2]I write to you as your apostolic father: If you think there is benefit

---

a 4:27 See Isaiah 54:1.
b 4:28 Or "royal proclamation."
c 4:30 See Genesis 21:10. This is showing that the two "sons" are not meant to live together.
   You cannot mingle law and grace, for only grace is based upon the promise of new life.
d 4:30 See Genesis 21:10–12; John 8:35.

in circumcision and Jewish regulations to make you holy,[a] then you're acting as though Jesus the Anointed One is not enough. [3]I say it again emphatically: Anyone who believes that circumcision brings them closer to God is obliged to fulfill every single one of the commandments and regulations of the Law!

[4]If you want to be made holy by fulfilling the obligations of the Law, you have cut off more than your flesh—you have cut yourselves off from the Anointed One and have fallen away from the revelation of grace!

[5]But the Holy Spirit convinces us that we have received by faith the glorious righteousness of the Anointed One. [6]When you're placed into the Anointed One and joined to him, circumcision and religious obligations can benefit you nothing. All that matters now is living in the faith that is activated and brought to perfection by love.

[7]Before you were led astray, you were so faithful to Messiah. Why have you now turned away from what is right and true? Who has deceived you?

[8]The One who enfolded you into his grace is not behind this false teaching that you've embraced. Not at all! [9]Don't you know that when you allow even a little lie into your heart, it can permeate your entire belief system?[b]

[10]Deep in my heart I have faith that the Lord Jesus the Anointed One, who lives in you, will bring you back around to the truth. And I'm convinced that those who agitate you, whoever they think they are, will be brought under God's judgment!

---

a 5:2 Implied in the context.
b 5:9 Literally "A little yeast goes through the whole lump of dough." The text uses a metaphor of "yeast" that has effects that cannot be hidden when it is folded into dough. The yeast is the lie of legalism.

¹¹Dear friends, why do you think the religious system persecutes me? Is it because I preach the message of being circumcised and keeping all the laws of Judaism? Not at all! Is there no longer any offense over the cross? ¹²To tell you the truth, I am so disgusted with all your agitators, who are obsessed with cutting—I wish they would go even further and cut off their legalistic influence from your lives![a]

¹³Beloved ones, God has called us to live a life of freedom in the Holy Spirit. But don't view this wonderful freedom as an opportunity to set up a base of operations in the natural realm. Freedom means that we become so completely free of self-indulgence that we become servants of one another, expressing love in all we do.

¹⁴For love completes the laws of God. All of the Law can be summarized in one grand statement:

"Demonstrate love to your neighbor,
even as you care for and love yourself."[b]

¹⁵But if you continue to criticize and come against each other over minor issues, you're acting like wild beasts trying to destroy one another![c]

¹⁶As you yield freely and fully to the dynamic life and power of the Holy Spirit, you will abandon the cravings of your self-life.[d] ¹⁷For your self-life craves the things that offend the Holy Spirit and hinder him from living free within you! And the Holy Spirit's intense cravings hinder your old self-life from dominating you! The Holy Spirit is the only One

---

a 5:12 Or "castrate themselves."
b 5:14 See Leviticus 19:18.
c 5:15 Both Aramaic and Greek manuscripts read "biting and devouring," which is a metaphor for critical attitudes that will destroy the fellowship. These terms were often found in classic Greek literature to describe wild animals fighting each other in deadly conflict.
d 5:16 Or "the natural realm."

who defeats the cravings of your natural life. So then, the two incompatible and conflicting forces within you are your self-life of the flesh and the new creation life of the Spirit.[a]

[18]But when you are brought into the full freedom of the Spirit of Grace, you will no longer be living under the domination of the law, but soaring above it![b]

[19]And what are the cravings of the self-life I'm referring to? They are obvious: Sexual immorality, lustful thoughts, pornography, [20]chasing after things instead of God,[c] manipulating others,[d] hatred of those who get in your way, senseless arguments, resentment when others are favored, temper tantrums, angry quarrels, only thinking of yourself, being in love with your own opinions, [21]being envious of the blessings of others, murder, uncontrolled addictions,[e] wild parties, and all other similar behavior.

Haven't I already warned you that those who use their "freedom" for these things[f] will not inherit the kingdom realm of God!

[22-23]But the fruit[g] produced by the Holy Spirit within you is divine.[h] This love is revealed through:

joy that overflows,[i]

peace that subdues,

---

a 5:17 The concept of the "new creation life of the Spirit" is implied in the greater context of Galatians, and referred to explicitly in 6:15–16.

b 5:18 Implied in the context. The word for Spirit is actually "Spirit-Wind."

c 5:20 Literally "idolatry."

d 5:20 Literally "witchcraft." The Greek word for "witchcraft" can imply drug usage.

e 5:20 Literally "drunken binges."

f 5:21 The Aramaic literally means "those who devote themselves to these things."

g 5:22–23 The Greek word here can be translated "harvest."

h 5:22–23 There is clear textual inference that the "fruit" (singular) of the Holy Spirit is love, with the other virtues displaying aspects of the greatest quality of Spirit-life, agape love.

i 5:22–23 The translator has chosen to add implied action to these virtues, for they are not meant to be abstract virtues, but made visible with actions.

patience that endures,[a]
kindness in action,[b]
a life full of virtue,[c]
faith that prevails,
gentleness of heart, and
strength of spirit.[d]
Never set the law above these qualities, for they are meant to be limitless.[e]

[24]Keep in mind that we who belong to Jesus, the Anointed One, have already experienced crucifixion. For everything connected with our self-life was put to death on the cross and crucified with Messiah. [25]We have now chosen to live in the surrendered freedom of yielding to the Holy Spirit![f] [26]So may we never be found dishonoring one another, or comparing ourselves to each other, for each of us is an original. We have forsaken all jealousy that diminishes the value of others.[g]

---

a 5:22-23 The Greek word for patience is taken from a verb that means "ever tapping" or "never quitting."

b 5:22-23 The Aramaic word is actually "sweetness."

c 5:22-23 Or "goodness."

d 5:22-23 Although the word *self* is not found in this verse, most translations render this as "self-control." The word is actually "lordship," or by implication "spirit-strength."

e 5:22-23 Literally "there is no law set against these things" or "there is no conflict with Jewish laws."

f 5:25 As translated from the Aramaic.

g 5:26 As translated from the Aramaic.

Six

—

¹My beloved friends, if you see a believer who is overtaken with a fault,ᵃ may the one who overflows with the Spiritᵇ seek to restore him to fellowship with the Anointed One. Win him over with gentle words, which will open his heart to you and will keep you from exalting yourself over him.ᶜ ²Love empowers us to fulfill the law of the Anointed One as we carry each other's troubles. ³If you think you are too important to stoop down to help another, you are living in deception.

⁴Let everyone be devoted to fulfill the work God has given them to do with excellence, and their joy will be in doing what's right and being themselves, and not in being affirmed by others. ⁵Every believer is ultimately responsible for his or her own conscience.ᵈ

⁶And those who are taught the Word will receive an impartationᵉ from their teacher; a sharing of wealthᶠ takes place between them.

⁷Make no mistake about it, God will never be mocked! For what you plant will always be the very thing you harvest. ⁸The harvest you reap reveals the seed that was planted.ᵍ If you plant the corrupt seeds of self-life into this natural realm, you can expect to experience a harvest of corruption. If you plant the good seedsʰ of Spirit-life you will reap the beautiful fruits that grow from the everlasting life of the Spirit.

---

a 6:1 Or "mistake."
b 6:1 Literally "those who are in the Spirit."
c 6:1 Or "keep you from being harassed by the enemy."
d 6:5 As translated from the Aramaic.
e 6:6 Or "blessings."
f 6:6 Literally "wealth."
g 6:8 Implied in the context.
h 6:8 These "good seeds" would include prayer, Bible study, speaking wise words, giving,

⁹And don't allow yourselves to be weary or disheartened in planting good seeds, for the season of reaping the wonderful harvest you've planted is coming! ¹⁰Take advantage of every opportunity to be a blessing to others,ᵃ especially to our brothers and sisters in the family of faith!

¹¹You must understand, I've written this letter to you with my own handwriting—see how large I have to make the letters?ᵇ ¹²All those who insist that you be circumcised are recruiting you so they can boast in their own works. They are attempting to avoid the persecution that comes with preaching the liberating message of the cross of Messiah! ¹³Not even those who are circumcised keep every detail of the written Law. Yet they push you to be circumcised so that they can boast that you have become like them.

¹⁴My only boast is in the crucifixion of the Lord Jesus, our Messiah. In him I have been crucified to this natural realm; and the natural realm is dead to me and no longer dominates my life.

¹⁵Circumcision doesn't mean a thing to me. The only thing that really matters is living by the transforming power of this wonderful new creation life. ¹⁶And all those who live in agreement with this standard will have true peace and God's delight, for they are the Israel of God.

¹⁷From now on, let no one bring me trouble or criticism, for I am carrying the very scarsᶜ of our Lord Jesus in my body. ¹⁸Finally my

---

loving, and dropping "seeds" every day from a life lived in our new creation life.

a 6:10 The Greek text implies giving finances.

b 6:11 Some Greek texts imply that only beginning with verse 11 does Paul write in his own handwriting. The Aramaic indicates the entire letter was written in his handwriting.

c 6:17 The Aramaic word for "scars" can also mean "death marks" or "stigmata."

beloved ones—may the wonderful grace of our Lord Jesus, the Anointed One, be flowing in your spirit.[a] So shall it be!

> In Messiah's love,
> Paul

---

a   6:18 Or "with your spirits."

Ephesians

HEAVEN'S RICHES

Translator's Introduction to Ephesians

AT A GLANCE

Author: The apostle Paul

Audience: The church of Ephesus, and surrounding area churches

Date: AD 60–62

Type of Literature: A letter

Major Themes: Salvation and grace, God's power, church unity, and Christian conduct and identity.

Outline:
Letter Opening — 1:1–2
The Church's Heavenly Calling — 1:3–3:21
The Church's Earthly Conduct — 4:1–6:20
Letter Closing — 6:21–24

ABOUT EPHESIANS

What you are about to read is meant to be taught to every church. It is the constitution of our faith, the great summary description of all that is precious and esteemed in Christian doctrine and Christian living.

Paul firmly plants the cornerstone of our faith in this powerful letter, cementing the position and authority of the church over every other force in its few pages. In it, Paul brings before every believer the mystery of the glory of Christ.

The theme of Ephesians is that God will one day submit everything under the leadership of Jesus Christ. He is the Head of the church and the fullness of God in human flesh. He gives his church extraordinary power to walk filled with the Holy Spirit, revealing the nature of God in all things. Jesus loves the church and cherishes everything about her. He is the one who brings Jews and non-Jews into one body. The church is God's new humanity—one new man. It is the new temple where God's glory dwells. And the church is the bride of Christ, the beloved partner who is destined to rule with him.

How wonderfully he blesses his bride with gifts from above. He gives us, both men and women, the grace to be apostles, prophets, evangelists, pastors, and teachers who will feed and encourage the church to rise higher. The greatness of God streams from Jesus Christ into the hearts of every believer. These are the grand themes of Ephesians.

I always loved the apostolic prayers of Paul, especially those found in Ephesians. I have prayed nearly every day for forty years that God would impart to me the spirit of revelation and the spirit of wisdom to guide my life, my family, and my ministry. God is good to give the Holy Spirit's fullness to those who ask with sincere hunger for more.

PURPOSE

What an exciting letter Paul has written to us! Ephesians is full of life and its words reach higher in Christian thought than any letter in our New

Testament. Full of living revelation, it simply drips with the anointing of the Holy Spirit. Where most of Paul's letters are addressed to churches facing specific issues dealing with belief and practice, this isn't the case with Ephesians. There is a more general, theologically reflective tone to this letter that is meant to ground, shape, and challenge general (mainly Gentile) believers in their faith.

AUTHOR AND AUDIENCE

Paul wrote this letter about AD 60, while in a prison cell in Rome, and sent it with Tychicus as a circular letter that was to be read to all the churches.

Originally, there were no titles on Paul's letters. They were gathered and the titles were assigned according to where they were sent; then they were published for the churches as a group. In none of the earliest Greek manuscripts did the word "Ephesus" or "Ephesians" occur. It was simply added in the margin next to the main text in the first copies made. The conclusion by some scholars is that this letter to the Ephesians may possibly be the lost letter of the Laodiceans mentioned in Colossians 4:16: "Once you've read this letter publicly to the church, please send it on to the church of the Laodiceans, and make sure you read the letter that I wrote to them." Others believe it was intended for Ephesus as it stands today.

Scholars are not sure on this point; it is the only letter Paul wrote that did not contain any personal greetings to specific people. Since these greetings easily identified the other letters, many now believe this letter was written not only for the Ephesians but for Christians in the surrounding area too.

MAJOR THEMES

Salvation by grace through faith. Paul paints a very bleak picture of who we were before God stepped in to rescue us: "you were once like corpses, dead in your sins and offenses" (2:1). Yet he goes on: "Even when we were dead and doomed in our many sins, he united us into the very life of Christ and saved us by his wonderful grace!" (2:4–5). Paul makes it clear we don't earn or work for this rescue; rather, it's God's undeserved favor from top to bottom!

Power of God over all others. One of the leading themes in this letter from heaven is the theme that God's power trumps that of all other principalities, powers, and authorities in this world. For Paul, any threat of the spiritual powers of this world should be seen in light of the superior power of God and the power we have as his children.

Christian unity. Another leading theme in Paul's letter is the unity that Jews and non-Jews share in Christ. Paul's strong encouragement for unity and love within the body work together to encourage believers to overcome any and all cultural pressures of animosity on the basis of Jesus' work uniting all believers into one community of people.

Christian conduct. Most of chapters 3–6 focus on how Christians should live, especially new believers, which is summed up with Paul's appeal in 4:17 to "not live like the unbelievers around you who walk in their empty delusions." Paul urges new believers—and really all believers—to cultivate a lifestyle consistent with their new life in Christ—a life free from drunkenness, sexual immorality, lying, stealing, bitterness, and other behaviors from their former life.

Christian identity. One of the major themes of Paul's teachings is the fact that believers are now "in Christ," an idea that impacts every aspect of believers' identity. We exist in a personal, energizing relationship of unity with the risen Christ! This identity is crucial in our ongoing struggle with spiritual darkness and powers, maintaining Christian unity, overcoming our former lifestyle, and living as God has called us to live.

———

See the wonder of God before your eyes. Drink in the sweetness of heavenly revelation and enjoy this most exhilarating letter from heaven—Ephesians!

One

———

Dear friends,

¹My name is Paul, and I was chosen by God to be an apostle of Jesus, the Messiah. ²I'm writing this letter to all the devoted believers[a] who have been made holy[b] by being one with Jesus, the Anointed One.

May God himself, the heavenly Father of our Lord Jesus Christ, release grace over you and impart total well-being into your lives.[c]

³Every spiritual blessing in the heavenly realm has already been lavished upon us as a love gift from our wonderful heavenly Father, the Father of our Lord Jesus—all because he sees us wrapped into Christ. This is why we celebrate[d] him with all our hearts!

⁴And he chose us to be his very own, joining us to himself even before he laid the foundation of the universe![e] Because of his great love, he ordained[f] us as one with Christ from the beginning, so that we would be seen as holy in his eyes with an unstained innocence.

---

a 1:2 Recent manuscripts add the words, "those who are in Ephesus." The oldest manuscripts have "to the Ephesians" written in the margin. This would reinforce the theory that it is meant to be read and distributed to all the churches. Although the book bears the name "Ephesians," some scholars believe that this letter could be the missing letter to the Laodiceans mentioned in Colossians 4:16. Regardless, Ephesians contains the most crucial truths for believers worldwide.

b 1:2 Or "To the saints (holy ones) and the faithful in Christ Jesus. Notice that God is the one who makes us holy, but our response is to be "faithful (devoted)."

c 1:2 Or "peace." The Hebrew concept of peace means much more than tranquility.

d 1:3 Or "Bless (blessed be God)."

e 1:4 As translated from the Aramaic. There is an alternate Greek translation of the unique wording of this verse that could be translated "He chose us to be a 'word' before the fall of the world." The Greek word for "chose" is *eklegomai*, which is a form of *lego* (speak). The word for "fall" (Adam's fall) is *kataboles*, which can mean "falling down," but is usually translated as "foundation (of the world)."

f 1:4 As translated from the Aramaic. One Eastern Aramaic text reads "He marked us with his love." The Greek text states "predestined us" or "set us apart."

⁵⁻⁶For it was always in his perfect plan*ᵃ* to adopt*ᵇ* us as his delightful children, through our union with Jesus, the Anointed One, so that his tremendous love that cascades over us would glorify his grace*ᶜ*—for the same love he has for his Beloved One, Jesus, he has for us. And this unfolding plan brings him great pleasure!

⁷Since we are now joined to Christ, we have been given the treasures of redemption by his blood—the total cancellation*ᵈ* of our sins—all because of the cascading riches of his grace.*ᵉ* ⁸This superabundant grace is already powerfully working in us,*ᶠ* releasing within us all forms of wisdom and practical understanding. ⁹And through the revelation of the Anointed One, he unveiled his secret desires to us—the hidden mystery of his long-range plan, which he was delighted to implement from the very beginning of time. ¹⁰And because of God's unfailing purpose, this detailed plan will reign supreme through every period of time until the fulfillment of all the ages finally reaches its climax—when God makes all things new*ᵍ* in all of heaven and earth through Jesus Christ.

¹¹Through our union with Christ we too have been claimed by God as his own inheritance.*ʰ* Before we were even born, he gave us our destiny;*ⁱ* that we would fulfill the plan of God who always accomplishes

---

a 1:5-6 Or "He marked out our horizon (destiny) beforehand."

b 1:5 The Aramaic reads "to establish us."

c 1:5-6 Or "to the praise of the glory of his grace."

d 1:7 Or "forgiveness." The Greek word, *aphesis, means* "to send away" or "to set free (from bondage)."

e 1:7 The Greek word for riches (*ploutos*) is also used to describe God's wisdom and knowledge in Romans 11:33. Just as God is all-knowing and has all-wisdom, so he has untold riches of grace available for God's children.

f 1:8 Or "lavished on us."

g 1:10 As translated from the Aramaic. The Greek text states "God will gather together all things in fulfillment in Christ." That is, God will unite all things under the headship of Christ.

h 1:11 The Greek construction of this phrase can mean either that God appointed us (Gr. *klēroō*, chosen by casting lots) to be his inheritance, or that we have been appointed an inheritance.

i 1:11 Or "estate."

every purpose and plan in his heart. ¹²God's purpose was that we *Jews*, who were the first to long for the messianic hope, would be the first to believe in the Anointed One and bring great praise and glory to God!

¹³And because of him, when you who are not Jewish heard the revelation*ᵃ* of truth, you believed in the wonderful news of salvation. Now we have been stamped with the seal of the promised Holy Spirit.*ᵇ*

¹⁴He is given to us like an engagement ring*ᶜ* is given to a bride, as the first installment of what's coming! He is our hope-promise of a future inheritance*ᵈ* for all who have been made alive in Christ. This hope-promise seals us until we have all of redemption's promises and experience complete freedom—all for the supreme glory and honor of God!

¹⁵Because of this, since I first heard about your strong faith in the Lord Jesus Christ and your tender love toward all his devoted ones, ¹⁶My heart is always full and overflowing with thanks to God for you as I constantly remember you in my prayers.*ᵉ* ¹⁷I pray that the Father of Glory, the God of our Lord Jesus Christ, would impart to you the riches of the Spirit of wisdom and the Spirit of revelation*ᶠ* to know him through your deepening intimacy with him.

¹⁸I pray that the light of God will illuminate the eyes of your imagination,*ᵍ* flooding you with light, until you experience the full revelation of the hope of his calling*ʰ*—that is, the wealth of God's glorious inheritances that he finds in us, his holy ones!

---

a   1:13 The Greek text is *Logos* or "Word of God."
b   1:13 Some Aramaic manuscripts add here "who was announced by the angels."
c   1:14 The Greek word used here can be translated "pledge," "down payment" or "engagement ring."
d   1:14 The Aramaic word used for "inheritance" can also be translated "dividend."
e   1:16 The literal Aramaic text reads "I began confessing on your behalf and praying."
f   1:17 Or "discovery."
g   1:18 Or "innermost (heart)."
h   1:18 Or "to which he is calling you."

[19]My prayer for you is that you will continually experience the immeasurable greatness of God's power made available to you through faith. Then your lives will be an advertisement of this immense power as it works through you! [20]This is the mighty resurrection power that was released when God raised Christ from the dead and exalted him[a] to the place of highest honor and supreme authority[b] in the heavenly realm! [21]And now he is exalted as first above every ruler, authority, government, and realm of power in existence! He is gloriously enthroned over every name that is ever praised,[c] not only in this age,[d] but in the age that is coming![e]

[22]And he alone is the Leader and Source of everything needed in the church. God has put everything beneath the authority of Jesus Christ[f] and has given him the highest rank above all others. [23]And now we, his church, are his body on the earth and that which fills him who is being filled by it![g]

Two
___

[1]*And his fullness fills you,* even though you were once like corpses,[h] dead in your sins and offenses. [2]It wasn't that long ago that you lived

---

a 1:20 Or "he seated him (enthroned)."

b 1:20 Or "at His right hand," a metaphor for the place of honor and authority.

c 1:21 As translated literally from the Aramaic.

d 1:21 The Aramaic word is actually "universe."

e 1:21 As translated literally from the Aramaic.

f 1:22 Both Greek and Aramaic texts use the figure of speech "under his feet," which means he has conquered, subdued, and now rules over them.

g 1:23 That is, as we are those who are filled (completed) by Christ, we also complete (fill) him. What a wonderful and humbling mystery is revealed by this verse.

h 2:1 As translated literally from the Greek.

in the religion, customs, and values[a] of this world,[b] obeying the dark ruler of the earthly realm who fills the atmosphere with his authority, and works diligently in the hearts of those who are disobedient to the truth of God. [3]The corruption that was in us from birth was expressed through the deeds and desires of our self-life. We lived by whatever our natural cravings and thoughts our minds dictated, living as rebellious children subject to God's wrath like everyone else.

[4]But God still loved us with such great love. He is so rich in compassion and mercy. [5]Even when we were dead and doomed in our many sins, he united us into the very life of Christ and saved us by his wonderful grace! [6]He raised us up with Christ the exalted One, and we ascended with him into the glorious perfection and authority[c] of the heavenly realm, for we are now co-seated as one with Christ!

[7]Throughout the coming ages[d] we will be the visible display of the infinite, limitless riches of his grace and kindness, which was showered upon us in Jesus Christ. [8]For it was only through this wonderful grace that we believed in him. Nothing we did could ever earn this salvation, for it was the gracious gift from God that brought us to Christ! [9]So no one will ever be able to boast, for salvation is never a reward for good works or human striving.

[10]We have become his poetry,[e] a re-created people that will fulfill the destiny he has given each of us, for we are joined to Jesus, the

---

a 2:2 The Aramaic literally means "the worldliness of this world."

b 2:2 The Aramaic phrase can also refer to the authority of secular governments.

c 2:6 Implied in the text. To be "placed" or "seated" in heaven means we have been given the perfection and authority to be there.

d 2:7 The Aramaic literally means "universes."

e 2:10 The beautiful Greek word used here is translated "poem" or "poetry." Our lives are the beautiful poetry written by God that will speak forth all that he desires in life.

Anointed One. Even before we were born, God planned in advance our destiny[a] and the good works we would do to fulfill it!

[11-12]So don't forget how far you've come. You were not born as Jews and were uncircumcised (circumcision itself is just a work of man's hands); you had none of the Jewish covenants and laws; you were foreigners to Israel's incredible heritage[b]; you were without the covenants and prophetic promises of the Messiah, the promised hope, and without God. You are found complete in the faith of Jesus the Messiah, all because of this glorious grace![c]

[13]Yet look at you now! Everything is new! Although you were once distant and far away from God, now you have been brought delightfully close to him through the sacred blood of Jesus—you have actually been united to Christ!

[14]Our reconciling "Peace" is Jesus! He has made Jew and non-Jew one in Christ. By dying as our sacrifice, he has broken down every wall of prejudice that separated us and has now made us equal through our union with Christ. [15]Ethnic hatred has been dissolved by the crucifixion of his precious body on the cross. The legal code that stood condemning every one of us has now been repealed by his command. His triune essence[d] has made peace between us by starting over—forming one new race of humanity,[e] Jews and non-Jews fused together!

[16]Two have now become one, and we live restored to God and reconciled in the body of Christ. Through his crucifixion, hatred died.

---

a 2:10 Although implied, these good works make up our destiny. As we yield to God, our prearranged destiny comes to pass and we are rewarded for simply doing what he wanted us to accomplish.

b 2:11-12 Or "freedom," or, "commonwealth."

c 2:12 This last phrase is implied in the context and is necessary to complete the English structure of thought.

d 2:15 As translated literally from the Aramaic. The Greek is, "to create in himself one new man."

e 2:15 Or "one new man."

[17]For the Messiah has come to preach this sweet message of peace to you,[a] the ones who were distant, and to those who are near. [18]And now, because we are united to Christ and to each other, we both have equal and direct access in the realm of the Holy Spirit to come before the Father!

[19]So, you are not foreigners or guests, even though you are non-Jewish, but rather you are the children of the city of the holy ones,[b] with all the rights as family members of the household of God. [20]You are rising like the perfectly fitted stones of the temple;[c] and your lives are being built up together upon the ideal foundation laid by the apostles and prophets, and best of all, you are connected to the Head Cornerstone of the building, the Anointed One, Jesus Christ himself!

[21]This entire building is under construction and is continually growing under his supervision until it rises up completed as the holy temple of the Lord himself. [22]This means that God is transforming each one of you into the Holy of Holies, his dwelling place, through the power of the Holy Spirit living in you!

Three

[1]Beloved friends, because of my love for Jesus Christ, I am now his prisoner for the sake of all of you who are not Jews. [2]I have been made his prisoner so that you will hear the gospel that God has entrusted to

---

a   2:17 This is Paul's paraphrase of Isaiah 57:19.
b   2:19 As translated literally from the Aramaic.
c   2:20 The "temple" is not found in the text here, but is explicitly mentioned in v. 21.

me to share with you in this letter. [3]For this wonderful mystery, which I briefly described, was given to me by divine revelation. I'm sharing it now with you in detail, [4]so that whenever you read it you will be able to understand my revelation and insight into the secret mystery of the Messiah.

[5]There has never been a generation that has been given the detailed understanding of this glorious and divine mystery until now. He kept it a secret until this generation. God is revealing it only now to his sacred apostles and prophets by the Holy Spirit. [6]Here's the secret he revealed to me: The gospel of grace has made you, non-Jewish believers, into coheirs of his promise of glory[a] through your union with him. And you have now become members of his body—one with the Anointed One, and one with each other![b]

[7-8]I have been made a messenger of this wonderful news by the gift of grace that works through me. Even though I am the least significant of all his holy believers, this grace-gift was imparted when the manifestation of his power came upon me. Grace alone empowers me so that I can boldly preach this wonderful message to non-Jewish people, sharing with them the unfading,[c] inexhaustible riches of Christ, which are beyond comprehension.

[9]God's grace fuels my passion to enlighten every person to this wonderful mystery, which was kept a secret in the heart of God, the Creator of all, and has been hidden from the world until now.

[10]And why did he do this? So that every throne and rank of angelic orders in the heavenly realm would have unveiled before their eyes

---

a   3:6 Implied in the context of Ephesians and Paul's letters. Both Greek and Aramaic manuscripts read only "the promise."

b   3:6 Implied in the context.

c   3:7-8 The word *unfading* comes from an Aramaic word which can also be translated "unquestionable" or "without fault." The Greek uses the word *unsearchable*.

God's full and diverse wisdom[a] revealed through his loving plan[b] for the church.[c] [11]This perfectly wise plan was destined from eternal ages and fulfilled completely in our Lord Jesus Christ, so that now [12]we have boldness through him,[d] and free access as kings[e] before the Father because of our complete confidence in Christ's faithfulness.

[13]My dear friends, I pray that you will remain strong and not be discouraged or ashamed by all that I suffer on your behalf, for it is for your glory. [14]So when I think of the wisdom of his plan I kneel humbly in awe before the Father of our Lord Jesus, the Messiah, [15]the perfect Father of every father and child[f] in heaven and on the earth. [16]And I pray that he would pour out over you the unlimited riches of his glory and favor until supernatural strength floods your innermost being with his divine might and explosive power.

[17]Then, by constantly using your faith, the life of Christ will be released deep inside you, and the resting place of his love will become the very source and root of your life, providing you with a secure foundation that grows and grows.

[18-19]Then, as your spiritual strength increases, you will be empowered to discover what every holy one experiences—the great magnitude[g] of the astonishing love of Christ in all its dimensions. How deeply

---

a 3:10 The Greek word used here can be translated "multi-colored wisdom."

b 3:10 Implied in the context.

c 3:10 The church is the "university of the angels" and every believer is a "professor" teaching the heavenly realm the mysteries and wonders of the grace of God. The angels investigate through our lives the treasures of grace, like the cherubim who gaze upon the mercy seat. See 1 Peter 1:12.

d 3:12 The Greek words used here can be translated, "freedom of speech to say whatever you want with boldness."

e 3:12 The Aramaic text can be translated "we have kingship."

f 3:15 Translated from the Aramaic. It could also be translated "the perfect Father of every people group." The Greek word for "father" and the word for "family" are quite similar, which indicates that every family finds its source in the Father.

g 3:18–19 Or "excellence."

intimate and far-reaching is his love! How enduring and inclusive it is! Endless love beyond measurement that transcends our understanding—this extravagant love pours into you until you are filled to overflowing with the fullness of God!

[20]Never doubt God's mighty power to work in you and accomplish all this. He will achieve infinitely more than your greatest request, your most unbelievable dream, and exceed your wildest imagination! He will outdo them all, for his miraculous power constantly energizes you.

[21]Now we offer up to God all the glorious praise that rises from every church in every generation through Jesus Christ—and all that will yet be manifest through time and eternity. Amen!

Four

[1]As a prisoner of the Lord,[a] I plead with you to walk holy, in a way that is suitable to your high rank, given to you in your divine calling. [2]With tender humility and quiet patience, always demonstrate gentleness and generous[b] love toward one another, especially toward those who may try your patience. [3]Be faithful to guard the sweet harmony of the Holy Spirit among you in the bonds of peace, [4]so that you will be one body and one spirit, as you were all called into the same glorious hope of divine destiny.

[5]For the Lord God is one, and so are we,[c] for we share in one faith,

---

a 4:1 Paul wrote this letter while a prisoner in Rome because of his faith in Christ. See Song of Songs 8:6 TPT.
b 4:2 The Aramaic word literally means "stretching."
c 4:5 Implied in the context of our unity in Christ.

one baptism, and one Father. ⁶And He is the perfect Father who leads us all, works through us all, and lives in us all! ⁷And he has generously given each one of us supernatural grace, according to the size of the gift of Christ. ⁸This is why he says:

> **"He ascends into the heavenly heights**
> **taking his many captured ones with him,**[a]
> **leading them in triumphal procession,**[b]
> **and gifts were given to men."**[c]

⁹⁻¹⁰Having first descended into hell,[d] he has ascended triumphantly into the heights of heaven to begin the restoration and fulfillment[e] of all things.[f]

¹¹And he has appointed some with grace to be apostles, and some with grace to be prophets, and some with grace to be evangelists,[g] and some with grace to be pastors,[h] and some with grace to be teachers.[i] ¹²And their calling is to nurture and prepare all the holy believers to do their own works of ministry, and as they do this they will enlarge and build up the body of Christ. ¹³These grace ministries will function until we all attain oneness in the faith, until we all experience the fullness of

---

a 4:8 Or "He captured captivity."

b 4:8 Implied in the text.

c 4:8 Or "men were given as gifts." See Psalm 68:18.

d 4:9–10 Or "So what is the meaning of 'he ascended,' except that he also descended to the lower regions, namely, the earth? He, is the very one who descended, is also the one who ascended above all the heavens, in order to fill all things." Both Greek and Aramaic texts are literally "the lower regions of the earth," which is a metaphor of hell.

e 4:9–10 As translated from the Aramaic. The Greek text says "that he might fill all things."

f 4:9–10 The translator has chosen to leave out the repetitive phrases found in these two verses, yet preserve the meaning.

g 4:11 The Aramaic literally means "preachers."

h 4:11 Or "shepherds."

i 4:11 The Aramaic literally means "wise orators."

what it means to know the Son of God,[a] and finally we become one perfect man[b] with the full dimensions of spiritual maturity and fully developed in the abundance of Christ.

[14]And then our immaturity will end! And we will not be easily shaken by trouble, nor led astray by novel teachings or by the false doctrines of deceivers[c] who teach clever lies that sound like the truth—only to pull us into their "flock." [15]But instead we will remain strong and always sincere in our love as we express the truth. All our direction and ministries will flow from Christ and lead us deeper into him, the anointed Head of his body, the church.

[16]For his "body" has been formed in his image and is closely joined together and constantly connected as one. And every member has been given divine gifts to contribute to the growth of all; and as these gifts operate effectively throughout the whole body, we are built up and made perfect in love.

[17]So with the wisdom given to me from the Lord I say: You should not live like the unbelievers around you who walk in their empty delusions.[d] [18]Their corrupted logic has been clouded because their hearts are so far from God—their blinded understanding and deep-seated moral darkness keeps them from the true knowledge of God. [19]Because of spiritual apathy, they cut themselves off from their only true hope, for they surrender their lives to lewdness, impurity, and sexual obsession.

[20]But this is not the way of life that Christ has unfolded within you. [21]If you have really experienced the Anointed One, and heard his

---

a   4:13 The Greek literally means "until we have the full knowledge of the Son of God."
b   4:13 The Hebrew and Aramaic word for perfect is gamar, and the word implies that perfection cannot come to the body of Christ without the example and teaching of these five ministries—apostles, prophets, evangelists, pastors, and teachers.
c   4:14 The Greek literally means "dice-playing gamblers."
d   4:17 Or "opinions."

truth, it will be seen in your life;[a] for we know that the ultimate reality[b] is embodied in Jesus!

[22]And he has taught you to let go of the lifestyle of the ancient man,[c] the old self-life, which was corrupted by sinful and deceitful desires that spring from delusions. [23]Now it's time to be made new by every revelation that's been given to you.[d] [24]And to be transformed as you embrace the glorious Christ-within as your new life and live in union with him! For God has re-created you all over again in his perfect righteousness, and you now belong to him in the realm of true holiness. [25]So discard every form of dishonesty and lying so that you will be known as one who always speaks the truth, for we all belong to one another in one body.

[26]So be passionate! But don't let the passion of your emotions[e] lead you to sin! Don't let anger control you or be fuel for revenge, not for even a day. [27]Don't give the slanderous accuser, the Devil, an opportunity to manipulate you! [28]If any one of you has stolen from someone else, never do it again. Instead, be industrious, earning an honest living, and then you'll have enough to bless those in need.

[29]And guard your speech—never let ugly or hateful words come from your mouth, but instead let your words become beautiful gifts[f] that encourage others; do this by speaking words of grace to help them.

[30]The Holy Spirit of God has sealed you in Jesus Christ until you experience your full salvation.[g] So never grieve the Spirit of God or take

a   4:21 Implied in the context.
b   4:21 Or "ultimate learning."
c   4:22 As translated from the Aramaic.
d   4:23 Or "in the spirit of your revelation."
e   4:26 The Aramaic word *ragza* means "to shake" or "tremble." It is a word used for any strong emotion, but usually refers to anger.
f   4:29 Or "constructive."
g   4:30 As translated from the Aramaic. The Greek text uses the word "salvation."

for granted his holy influence in your life.[a] [31]Lay aside bitter words, temper tantrums, revenge, profanity, and insults. [32]But instead be kind[b] and affectionate toward one another. Has God graciously forgiven you? Then graciously forgive one another in the depths of Christ's love.

Five

[1]Commit yourselves to becoming more like God and copy him in everything you do,[c] for then you will represent your Father as his beloved sons and daughters. [2]And continue to walk surrendered to the extravagant love of Christ, for he surrendered his life as a sacrifice for us. His great love for us was pleasing to God, like an aroma of adoration—a sweet healing fragrance[d] in heaven and earth.

[3]And have nothing to do with sexual immorality, lust, or greed—for you are his holy ones and let no one be able to accuse you of them in any form. [4]Guard your speech. Forsake obscenities and worthless insults; these are nonsensical words that bring disgrace and are unnecessary. Instead, let worship fill your heart and spill out in your words as you remind each other of God's goodness.

[5]For it has been made clear to you already that the kingdom of God cannot be accessed by anyone who is guilty of sexual sin, or who is impure

---

a 4:30 The Greek manuscripts have "do not grieve," while the Aramaic text reads "do not limit his scope." This translation includes both concepts.

b 4:32 The Aramaic word for "kind" can also be translated "sweet."

c 5:1 The Greek word *mimetes* frequently depicts an actor playing a role. God wants us to mimic him and be filled with his thoughts, his love, his deeds, his character.

d 5:2 The Aramaic word "fragrance" can also be translated "healing balm."

or greedy—for greed is the essence of idolatry. How could they expect to have an inheritance in Christ's kingdom while doing those things?

⁶Don't be fooled by those who speak their empty words and deceptive teachings telling you otherwise. This is what brings God's anger upon the rebellious! ⁷Don't listen to them or live like them at all. ⁸Once your life was full of sin's darkness, but now you have the very light of our Lord shining through you because of your union with him. Your mission is to live as children flooded with his revelation-light! ⁹And the supernatural fruits of his light[a] will be seen in you—goodness, righteousness, and truth. ¹⁰Then you will learn to choose what is beautiful to our Lord.

¹¹And don't even associate with the servants of darkness because they have no fruit in them; instead, reveal truth to them. ¹²The very things they do in secret are too vile and filthy to even mention. ¹³Whatever the revelation-light exposes, it will also correct, and everything that reveals truth is light to the soul.[b] ¹⁴This is why the Scripture says,

**"Arise, you sleeper! Rise up from the dead and the Anointed
One will shine his light into you!"[c]**

¹⁵⁻¹⁶So be very careful how you live, not being foolish as those with no understanding, but live honorably with true wisdom, for we are living in evil times. Take full advantage of every day as you spend your life for his purposes. ¹⁷And then you will have discernment to fully understand God's will. ¹⁸And don't get drunk with wine, which is rebellion;[d] instead be filled with the fullness of the Holy Spirit.[e] ¹⁹And your hearts

---

a 5:9 Some Greek manuscripts have "Spirit."
b 5:13 Or "everything revealed becomes light."
c 5:14 See Isaiah 26:19; 51:17; 52:1; 60:1.
d 5:18 The Aramaic literally means "the wine of the prodigal." The Greek is, "reckless living," or, "debauchery."
e 5:18 Or "be inebriated in the Spirit's fullness."

will overflow with a joyful song to the Lord Jehovah. Keep speaking to each other with words of Scripture, singing the Psalms with praises and spontaneous songs given by the Spirit![a] [20]Always give thanks to Father God for every person[b] he brings into your life in the name of our Lord Jesus Christ. [21]And you honor Christ by yielding to one another. Be tenderly devoted to each other in love. [22]For wives, this means being tenderly devoted[c] to your husbands like you are tenderly devoted to our Lord, [23]for the husband provides leadership for the wife, just as Christ provides leadership for his church, as the Savior and Reviver[d] of the body. [24]In the same way the church is devoted to Christ, let the wives be devoted to their husbands in everything.

[25]And to the husbands, you are to demonstrate love for your wives with the same tender devotion that Christ demonstrated to us, his bride.[e] For he died for us, sacrificing himself [26]to make us holy and pure, cleansing us through the showering of the pure water of the Word of God. [27]All that he does in us is designed to make us a mature church for his pleasure, until we become a source of praise to him—glorious and radiant,[f] beautiful and holy, without fault or flaw;[g] a bride fully prepared for him.

[28]Husbands have the obligation of loving and caring for their wives the same way they love and care for their own bodies, for to love your

---

a 5:19 Or "spiritual songs." There is no other song more spiritual than the Song of Songs. Perhaps Paul was encouraging the church to sing and rejoice in the greatest of all songs.

b 5:20 The Greek text is ambiguous; it can mean "give thanks for all things" or "for all people." The Aramaic is quite specific—"for all people." The phrase, "that [God] brings into your life," is implied.

c 5:22 As translated from the Aramaic. The Greek is "submit."

d 5:23 The Aramaic word used here can be translated "Savior" or "Reviver." This translation includes both concepts.

e 5:25 Or "church."

f 5:27 The Greek word for radiance (endoxos) can also mean "gorgeous, honorable, esteemed, splendid, infused with glory!" This is what Christ's love will do to you. See Strong's Concordance 1741.

g 5:27 The Greek text has "without any wrinkle." The Aramaic literally means "without chips or knots."

wife is to love your own self. [29]No one abuses his own body, but pampers it—serving and satisfying its needs. That's exactly what Christ, our example, does for his church! [30]He serves and satisfies us[a] as members of his body—his flesh and bones.

[31]For this reason a man is to leave his father and his mother and lovingly hold to his wife, since the two have become joined as one flesh.[b] [32]Marriage is the beautiful design of the Almighty,[c] a great and sacred mystery—meant to be a vivid example of Christ and his church. [33]So every married man should be gracious to his wife just as he is gracious to himself. And every wife should be tenderly devoted to her husband.

Six

[1]Children, if you want to be wise, listen to your parents and do what they tell you, and the Lord[d] will help you.

[2]For the commandment, "Honor your father and your mother," was the first of the Ten Commandments[e] with a promise attached: [3]"You will prosper[f] and live a long, full life if you honor your parents."

[4]Fathers, don't exasperate your children to anger,[g] but raise them up with loving discipline and counsel that brings the revelation of our Lord.

---

a   5:30 Inferred from verse 29 and made explicit here.
b   5:31 See Genesis 2:24.
c   5:32 As translated from the Aramaic
d   6:1 Or "through our Lord."
e   6:2 Implied in the text.
f   6:3 Or "it will go beautifully for you."
g   6:4 In other words, fathers should show consideration for the different levels of understanding

⁵Those who are employed should listen to their employers[a] and obey their instructions with great respect and honor.[b] Serve them with humility in your hearts as though you were working for the Master.[c]

⁶Always do what is right and not only when others are watching, so that you may please Christ as his servants by doing his will. ⁷Serve[d] your employers wholeheartedly and with love, as though you were serving Christ and not men. ⁸Be assured that anything you do that is beautiful and excellent will be repaid by our Lord, whether you are an employee or an employer.

⁹And to the caretakers of the flock[e] I say, do what is right with your people by forgiving them when they offend you, for you know there is a Master in heaven that shows no favoritism.

¹⁰Now my beloved ones, I have saved these most important truths for last: Be supernaturally infused with strength through your life-union with the Lord Jesus. Stand victorious with the force[f] of his explosive power flowing in and through you.

¹¹Put on God's complete armor provided for us, so that you will be protected as you fight against the evil strategies of the accuser![g] ¹²Your hand-to-hand combat is not with human beings, but with the highest principalities and authorities operating in rebellion under the heavenly

---

and experience that children possess, dealing with them at their level, or risk causing them loads of heartache.

a   6:5 Literally "servants should obey their caretakers."

b   6:5 Or "with trembling."

c   6:5 Or "the Messiah."

d   6:7 Or "minister to them."

e   6:9 As translated literally from the Aramaic. The "caretakers of the flock" can refer to both leadership in the church and in the workplace. The Greek text states "masters, do the same things to them, and give up threatening."

f   6:10 Or "weapons."

g   6:11 Or "the Devil."

realms.[a] For they are a powerful class of demon-gods[b] and evil spirits that hold[c] this dark world in bondage. [13]Because of this, you must wear all the armor that God provides so you're protected as you confront the slanderer,[d] for you are destined for all things[e] and will rise victorious.

[14]Put on truth as a belt to strengthen you to stand in triumph. Put on holiness as the protective armor that covers your heart. [15]Stand on your feet alert, then you'll always be ready to share the blessings of peace as you subdue your enemies.[f]

[16]In every battle, take faith as your wrap-around shield, for it is able to extinguish the blazing arrows coming at you from the evil one![g] [17-18]Embrace the power of salvation's full deliverance, like a helmet to protect your thoughts from lies. And take the mighty razor-sharp Spirit-sword[h] of the spoken Word of God.

Pray passionately[i] in the Spirit, as you constantly intercede with every form of prayer at all times. Pray the blessings of God upon all his believers.[19]And pray also that God's revelation would be released through me every time I preach the wonderful mystery of the hope-filled gospel. [20]Yes, pray that I may preach the wonderful news of God's kingdom with bold freedom at every opportunity. Even though I am chained as a prisoner, I am his ambassador.

---

a 6:12 Or literally "under heaven."
b 6:12 The classical Greek word used here is often used to refer to conjuring up pagan deities—supreme powers of darkness mentioned in occult rituals.
c 6:12 Or "possessors of this dark world."
d 6:13 Or "Devil."
e 6:13 As translated from the Aramaic. The Greek text can be translated "after you have conquered, you can stand in victory."
f 6:15 The last phrase is implied in the text.
g 6:16 The poetic language Paul uses here is likely a reference to Psalm 91:4–5.
h 6:17-18 This is the Greek word, *machaira*, which was a razor sharp Roman sword used in close combat.
i 6:17–18 Or "all desires."

²¹⁻²²I am sending you a dear friend, Tychicus, because I care so deeply about each of you.ᵃ He is a beloved brother and trustworthy minister in our Lord Jesus. He will share with you all the concerns that I have for your welfare and will inform you of how I am getting along. And he will also prophesy over youᵇ to encourage your hearts. ²³So may God shower his peace upon you, my beloved friends. And may the blessings of faith and love fill your hearts from God the Father and from our Lord Jesus, the Messiah. ²⁴Abundant grace will be with you all as each of you love our Lord Jesus Christ without corruption. Amen!

Love in Christ,
Paul

---

a 6:21–22 Tychicus, whose name means "child of fortune," is believed to be an Ephesian who took this letter, as Paul's representative, to the churches throughout Turkey. He is mentioned five times in the New Testament. See Acts 20:4; Colossians 4:7; 2 Timothy 4:12; and Titus 3:12.

b 6:21–22 Translated literally from the Aramaic. Prophecy in the local church will always encourage, edify, and enlighten. See 1 Corinthians 14:3.

Philippians

HEAVEN'S JOY

Translator's Introduction to Philippians

AT A GLANCE

Author: The apostle Paul

Audience: The church of Philippi

Date: AD 60–62

Type of Literature: A letter

Major Themes: The gospel, Christ's lordship, Christian conduct, and Christ's community and identity.

Outline:

Letter Opening — 1:1–11
Paul's Gospel Priority — 1:12–26
Gospel-Living Conduct — 1:27–2:18
Examples of Gospel-Living — 2:19–30
Paul's Gospel Experience — 3:1–21
Final Encouragements — 4:1–9
Letter Closing 4:10–23

ABOUT PHILIPPIANS

What joy and glory came out of Paul's prison cell! Most of us would be thinking of ourselves and how we could get out; but Paul wanted to send to the Philippian church the revelation of joy!

The church of Philippi began because of a supernatural vision experienced by Paul while he was ministering at Troas (Acts 16:8–10). He had a vision in the night of a man from Macedonia who stood at his bedside pleading with him to come and give them the gospel.

It was in Philippi that Paul was arrested for preaching the gospel. Thrown in a prison cell and beaten, he and his coworker Silas began to sing songs of joy and praise to the Most High God! This caused a tremendous miracle as the prison doors were flung open and they escaped—but not before leading their jailor to Christ!

Perhaps the jailor was the very man Paul had seen in his vision.

Philippi is where Paul met Lydia, a businesswoman who apparently led an import/export business from that city. The miracles of God birthed a church among the Philippians, and Paul longs to encourage them to never give up and to keep rejoicing in all things.

Paul's words point us to heaven. He teaches us that our true life is not only in this world, but it is in the heavenly calling, the heavenly realm, and in our heavenly life that was given to us through Christ, the heavenly Man. He left heaven to redeem us and reveal the heart of God, the heart of a servant. He gave us new birth that we would be heavenly lights in this dark world as witnesses of Christ's power to change our lives.

There is a good and glorious work that Christ has begun in our hearts and promises to complete until he is fully unveiled. Philippians teaches us how important it is to be joyful throughout our journey of becoming like Christ. The words *joy* and *rejoicing* occur eighteen times in this book. So read this heavenly letter of joy and be encouraged.

PURPOSE

This could be considered a letter written to friends. Throughout his Philippian letter, Paul speaks of unity and teaches how the church should live as one in the fellowship of Jesus Christ. We also discover in this, the warmest of Paul's letters, many truths about Jesus Christ, his humiliation and exaltation on high. Paul tells us that God seated us in the heavenly realm in his place of authority and power. No wonder we should have joy in our hearts!

AUTHOR AND AUDIENCE

Paul wrote this letter of heavenly joy about AD 60, while Timothy was visiting him in prison. Carried by one of the Philippian church leaders, Epaphroditus, it was delivered to the believers to be read publicly to all. He also wrote it to friends, to partners in the gospel, in the city of Philippi. Paul was motivated to write to these friends because of concerns he had over their disunity, suffering, and opponents. There were also two aspects of his imprisonment that cause him to write the letter: the gospel's advance while he was kept in chains, as well as the gift from the Philippian church. He wrote this letter to express his joyful faith in Christ Jesus while in prison and to communicate his appreciation and love for his generous friends in Philippi.

MAJOR THEMES

The gospel of Christ. Paul's main theme in this letter is the gospel, a word that appears more often in this letter than any of his other letters. He is specifically concerned with believers' ongoing relationship with

Christ on the other side of their acceptance of the gospel. He is also concerned with the advancement of the gospel, that Jesus' story of rescue and forgiveness goes out into all the world.

The lordship of Christ. At the heart of this letter is the famed *Christ Hymn* (2:6–11)—a soaring melody of worship, adoration, and revelation of the majesty and superiority of Christ as Lord over all. This hymn expresses in lofty, lyrical language the story of Jesus from his pre-existent glory to the universal praise of him as Lord paved by his obedience to death on the cross.

The conduct of Christ. Those who have received and believed the gospel are called to live according to the gospel, to conduct their lives in such a way that they live for Christ. For Paul, such a life is a process of seizing the surpassing worth of Christ and being seized by him. It is also a progressive pursuit of Christ in which we daily die with him in order to experience the fullness of his new life.

The community of Christ. The community of Christ is the new people of God. Paul contrasts this new people with those in the old community who tried to bring non-Jewish Christians into the circle of Judaism. He also contrasts this community with the world, reminding believers that we are citizens of heaven who submit to the lordship of Christ. Finally, he reminds believers of their unity as brothers and sisters within God's household.

———

I encourage you to memorize some of the following verses and let others know that Jesus is the one who makes every heart sing, flooding us with a bliss that cannot be restrained. Here is the heavenly letter of joy—Philippians. Enjoy!

One

———

Dear friends in Philippi,

[1-2]My name is Paul and I'm joined by Timothy,[a] both of us servants of Jesus, the Anointed One. We write this letter to all his devoted followers in your city, including your pastors,[b] and to all the servant-leaders[c] of the church.

May the blessings of divine grace and supernatural peace that flow from God our wonderful Father, and our Messiah, the Lord Jesus, be upon your lives.

[3-4]My prayers for you are full of praise to God as I give him thanks for you with great joy! I'm so grateful for our union together[d] in Christ [5]and our enduring partnership that began the first time I presented to you the gospel. [6]I pray with great faith for you, because I'm fully convinced that the One who began this glorious work[e] in you will faithfully continue the process of maturing you[f] and will put his finishing touches to it until the unveiling[g] of our Lord Jesus Christ!

[7]It's no wonder I pray with such confidence, since you have a

---

a 1:1-2 Timothy was Paul's convert, coworker, and spiritual son. See 1 Timothy 1:2.

b 1:1-2 Or "guardians," as translated from the Greek. The Aramaic text uses the word "priests," and could refer to Jewish priests who had received Jesus as the Messiah.

c 1:1-2 As translated from the Aramaic. The Greek text is "deacons." The word for deacon is actually taken from a Greek compound of the words *dia* and *kovis* that means "to kick up the dust," referring to a servant who is so swift to accomplish his service that he stirs up the dust of the street running to fulfill his duty.

d 1:3-4 Implied in the context.

e 1:6 Or "good (worthwhile) work." Paul uses language here that sounds similar to Genesis 1:2. When God created the heavens and the earth, he declared it to be "good." And now with the new creation life within us, God again sees our growth in grace as something good.

f 1:6 Or "He will see to it that you remain faithful."

g 1:6 Literally "day of Christ." This is the day of his unveiling, his appearing.

permanent place in my heart![a] You have remained partners with me in the wonderful grace *of God* even though I'm here in chains for standing up for the truth of the gospel.[b] [8]Only God knows how much I dearly love you with the tender affection[c] of Jesus, the Anointed One.

[9]I continue to pray for your love to grow and increase beyond measure, bringing you into the rich revelation of spiritual insight[d] in all things.

[10]This will enable you to choose[e] the most excellent way of all[f]— becoming pure and without offense until the unveiling of Christ.[g] [11]And you will be filled completely with the fruits of righteousness[h] that are found in Jesus, the Anointed One—bringing great praise and glory to God!

[12]I want you to know, dear ones,[i] what has happened to me has not hindered, but helped my ministry of preaching the gospel, causing it to expand and spread to many people. [13]For now the elite Roman

---

a 1:7 Or "since you have given me a permanent place in your hearts."

b 1:7 The Aramaic literally means "the truth of God's revelation." The Greek can also be translated "for the defense and proof (a possible hendiadys) of the gospel."

c 1:8 Or "mercies."

d 1:9 The Greek word for *insight* (aisthēsis) is a *hapax legomenon* in the NT and used numerous times in the LXX referring to practical understanding linked to life. It is a word that implies walking out the truth that insight reveals. It could also be translated "experience." Many translations render it "discernment," yet it is more than discerning something—it means to experience the reality of something and apply it to life.

e 1:10 The Greek word for *choose* (dokimazō) means "to examine, to discern, or approve after testing." It comes from a root word that means "accepted" or "pleasing." So discernment becomes the path to finding what God approves, not simply what God forbids. When love, revelation, and insight overflow into our discernment, we will always be looking for what is excellent and pleasing in God's eyes. We choose what is best, not by law or rules, but by loving discernment.

f 1:10 As translated from the Greek. The Aramaic literally means "choose those things that bring contentment."

g 1:10 Or "in preparation for the day of Christ." This is the day of his unveiling at his appearing.

h 1:11 Or "the fruit that is righteousness."

i 1:12 Or "my brothers."

guards and government officials[a] overseeing my imprisonment have plainly recognized that I am here because of my love for the Anointed One. [14]And what I'm going through has actually caused many believers[b] to become even more courageous in the Lord to be bold and passionate to preach the Word of God, all because of my chains.

[15]It's true that there are some who preach Christ out of competition and controversy, for they are jealous over the way God has used me.[c] Many others have purer motives—they preach with grace and love filling their hearts,[d] [16]because they know I've been destined for the purpose of defending the revelation of God.[e]

[17]Those who preach Christ with ambition and competition are insincere—they just want to add to the hardships of my imprisonment. [18]Yet in spite of all of this I am overjoyed! For what does it matter as long as Christ is being preached? If they preach him with mixed motives or with genuine love, the message of Christ is still being preached.

[19]*And I will continue to rejoice* because I know that the lavish supply[f] of the Spirit of Jesus, the Anointed One, and your intercession for me will bring about my deliverance.[g] [20]No matter what, I will continue to hope and passionately cling[h] to Christ, so that he will be openly revealed

---

a   1:13 Or "Caesar's court."
b   Or "brothers."
c   1:15 Implied in the text.
d   1:15 Or "with goodwill." The translation has borrowed the term "love" from v. 16 and made it explicit here as the purest motive for preaching the gospel.
e   1:16 As translated from the Aramaic. The Greek is "the gospel." The implication from the Aramaic is that some of these preachers had been ordained by Paul.
f   1:19 The Greek word for "supply" can also be translated "festive chorus."
g   1:19 A quotation from LXX of Job 13:16.
h   1:20 The Greek word is *apokaradokia* and can be translated "with the deepest and intense yearnings," or "the concentrated desire that abandons all other interests with outstretched hands in expectation." It is possible that Paul uses the words "passionately cling," and "hope" as a hendiadys (i.e. "my hope-filled intense expectation"). Romans 8:19 is the only other place in the New Testament where *apokaradokia* is found.

through me before everyone's eyes.[a] So I will not be ashamed![b] In my life or in my death, Christ will be magnified in me. [21]My true life is the Anointed One, and dying means gaining more of him.

[22-24]So here's my dilemma: Each day I live means bearing more fruit in my ministry; yet I fervently long to be liberated from this body[c] and joined fully to Christ. That would suit me fine, but the greatest advantage to you would be that I remain alive. So you can see why I'm torn between the two—I don't know which I prefer.

[25]Yet deep in my heart I'm confident that I will be spared so I can add to your joy and further strengthen and mature your faith.[d] [26]When I am freed to come to you, my deliverance will give you a reason to boast even more in Jesus Christ.

[27]Whatever happens, keep living your lives based on the reality of the gospel of Christ, *which reveals him to others*. Then when I come to see you, or hear good reports of you, I'll know that you stand united in one Spirit and one passion—celebrating together as conquerors[e] in the faith of the gospel.[f] [28]And then you will never be shaken or intimidated by the opposition that rises up against us, for your courage will only prove as a sure sign from God of their coming destruction and that you have found a new life.[g] [29]For God has graciously given you the privilege not only to believe in Christ, but also to suffer for him. [30]For you

---

a 1:20 Literally "with uncovered faces." Some interpret it to mean without shame.

b 1:20 See also Rom.1:16; 2 Cor. 10:8; 1 Pet. 4:16; and 1 Jn. 2:28.

c 1:22-24 The Greek uses the word analyō, which means "to fold up a tent and depart." Sailors used this word to say, "loose the ship and set sail." And farmers used analyō for "to unyoke an oxen (set it free)."

d 1:25 Or "that I could help with your pioneer advance and joy in faith." Paul was excited to help them make new pioneer advances in their faith and joy.

e 1:27 As translated literally from the Aramaic. The Greek states "striving side by side with one mind."

f 1:27 Or "his revelation."

g 1:28 Implied in the context.

have been called by him to endure the conflict in the same way I have endured it. We're in this fight together until we win the prize—for you know I'm not giving up.

Two

¹Look at how much encouragement[a] you've found in your relationship with the Anointed One! You are filled to overflowing with his comforting love. You have experienced a deepening friendship with the Holy Spirit and have felt his tender affection and mercy.[b]

²So I'm asking you, my friends, that you be joined together in perfect unity—with one heart, one passion, and united in one love. Walk together[c] with one harmonious purpose and you will fill my heart with unbounded joy.

³Be free from pride-filled opinions, *for they will only harm your cherished unity.* Don't allow self-promotion to hide in your hearts, but in authentic humility put others first and view others as more important than yourselves. ⁴Abandon every display of selfishness. Possess a greater concern for what matters to others instead of your own interests. ⁵And consider the example that Jesus, the Anointed One, has set before us. Let his mindset become your motivation.

⁶He existed in the form of God, yet he gave no thought to seizing equality with God as his supreme prize.[d] ⁷Instead he emptied himself of

---

a 2:1 The Greek word *paraklesis* can also mean "exhortation" or "comfort."
b 2:1 Or "sympathies." The Aramaic literally means "your heart flutters with his compassion."
c 2:2 Or "Be like-minded."
d 2:6 Or "as something to be exploited."

his outward glory by reducing himself to the form of a lowly Servant. He became human! [8]He humbled himself and became vulnerable, choosing to be revealed as a Man. He listened to the Father and was obedient to everything he heard.[a] He was a perfect example, even in his death—a criminal's death by crucifixion![b]

[9]Because of that obedience, God exalted him and multiplied his greatness! He has now been given the greatest of all names!

[10]The authority of the name of Jesus causes every knee to bow in reverence! Everything and everyone will one day submit to this name—in the heavenly realm, in the earthly realm, and in the demonic realm.[c] [11]And every tongue will proclaim in every language: "Jesus Christ is Lord Yahweh,"[d] bringing glory and honor to God, his Father![e]

[12]My beloved ones, just like you've always listened to everything I've taught you in the past, I'm asking you now to keep following my instructions as though I were right there with you. Now you must continue to make this new life fully manifested as you live[f] in the holy awe

---

a   2:8 Implied in the text. See also John 5:19.

b   2:8 Notice the seven steps Christ took from the throne to the cross in vv. 7–8: 1) He emptied himself. 2) He became a servant. 3) He became human. 4) He humbled himself. 5) He became vulnerable and revealed as a Man. 6) He was obedient until his death. 7) He died a criminal's death on the cross.

c   2:10 Or "heaven, earth, and under the earth." Some have interpreted "under the earth."

d   2:11 As translated from the Aramaic. The Greek text uses the word kurios, which is not the highest name for God. Yahweh (Hebrew) or Jehovah (Latin) is the highest name. Kurios is a title also used for false gods, land owners, merchants, and nobles. The Greek language has no equal to the sacred name (the tetragrammaton–YHWH), Yahweh. Only Hebrew and Aramaic have that equivalent. This verse makes it clear that the name given to Jesus at his exaltation was "Lord Jehovah" or "Lord Yahweh." The Hebrew name for Jesus is Yeshua (literally "God is a Saving-Cry"), which bears and reveals the name Yahweh. Jesus carries the name and reputation of his Father, Yahweh, within him. See John 17:11.

e   2:11 Note the seven steps of exaltation that God gave Jesus after the cross: 1) God exalted him and multiplied his greatness. 2) He possess the greatest name of all. 3) His sovereign authority will cause every knee to bow. 4) God decreed that everyone in heaven will bow in worship of the God-Man. 5) God decreed that every demonic being will bow to the God-Man. 6) God decreed that every tongue will proclaim that Jesus Christ is Lord Yahweh! 7) God received the glory and honor of sharing his throne with the God-Man.

f   2:12 The Aramaic literally means "push through the service of your life" or "work the work of

of God—which brings you trembling into his presence. [13]God will continually revitalize you, implanting within you the passion to accomplish the good things you desire to do.[a]

[14]Live a cheerful life, without complaining or division among yourselves. [15]For then you will be seen as innocent,[b] faultless, and pure children of God, even though you live in the midst of a brutal and perverse culture.[c] For you will appear among them as shining lights[d] in the universe, [16]offering them the words of eternal life.[e]

You are living proof that I haven't labored among you for nothing. Your lives are the fruit of my ministry and will be my glorious boast at the unveiling[f] of Christ!

[17]But I will rejoice even if my life is poured out like a liquid offering to God over your sacrificial and surrendered lives of faith.[g] [18]And so no matter what happens to me, you should rejoice in ecstatic celebration with me!

[19]Yet I'm trusting in our Lord Jesus that I may send Timothy to you soon, so I can be refreshed when I find out how you're doing. [20]Timothy is like no other, a coworker who stands faithful at all times. He carries the same passion for your welfare that I carry in my heart. [21]For it seems as though everyone else is busy seeking what is best for themselves

---

your life."
a   2:13 As translated from the Aramaic. The Greek is "to do his pleasure."
b   2:15 Or "mature."
c   2:15 See Deut. 32:5–6.
d   2:15 The Aramaic literally means "the enlightened ones."
e   2:16 The Aramaic literally means "you stand in the place of life to them." The Greek text means "holding out to them the word of life."
f   2:16 Or "day."
g   2:17 The interpretation of this verse is difficult; it is speaking about Paul's willingness to be a love offering for the Philippians if that's what God desired. There is a powerful figure of speech contained in the Aramaic, literally translated as "though I imbibe the wine poured over the offering." This is a metaphor of Paul shedding his blood one day because of his love for the Philippians. Indeed, Paul was later martyred for his faith.

instead of the things that are most important to our Lord Jesus Christ. [22]You already know about his excellent reputation, since he has served alongside me as a loyal son in the work of ministry. [23]After I see what transpires with me he's the one I will send to you to bless you. [24]And I'm trusting in my Lord to return to you in due time.

[25]But for now, I feel a stirring in my heart to send Epaphroditus[a] back to you immediately. He's a friend to me and a wonderful brother and fellow soldier who has worked with me as we serve as ministers of the gospel. And you sent him as your apostle to minister to me in my need. [26]But now he is grieved to know that you found out he had been sick, so he longs to return and comfort you in this.

[27]It's true he almost died, but God showed him mercy and healed him. And I'm so thankful to God for his healing, as I was spared from having the sorrow of losing him on top of all my other troubles! [28]So you can see why I'm delighted to send him to you now. I know that you're anxious to see him and rejoice in his healing, and it encourages me to know how happy you'll be to have him back.

[29]So warmly welcome him home in the Lord,[b] with joyous love, and esteem him highly, for people like him deserve it. [30]Because of me, he put his life on the line, despising the danger, so that he could provide for me with what you couldn't, since you were so far away. And he did it all because of his ministry for Christ.

---

a   2:25 His name means "charming."
b   2:29 Or "Lord Yahweh."

Three

———

¹My beloved ones, don't ever limit your joy or fail to rejoice in the wonderful experience of knowing our Lord Jesus!

I don't mind repeating what I've already written you because it protects you—²beware of those religious hypocrites[a] who teach that you should be circumcised to please God. ³For we have already experienced "heart-circumcision," and we worship God in the power and freedom of the Holy Spirit, not in laws and religious duties. We are those who boast in what Jesus Christ has done, and not in what we can accomplish in our own strength.

⁴It's true that I once relied on all that I had become. I had a reason to boast and impress people with my accomplishments—more than others—⁵for my pedigree was impeccable. I was born a true Hebrew of the heritage of Israel[b] as the son of a Jewish man from the tribe of Benjamin.[c] I was circumcised eight days after my birth and was raised in the strict tradition of Orthodox Judaism, living a separated[d] and devout life as a Pharisee. ⁶And concerning the righteousness of the Torah,[e] no one surpassed me; I was without a peer. Furthermore, as a fiery defender of the truth, I persecuted the messianic believers with religious zeal.

⁷Yet all of the accomplishments that I once took credit for, I've now

---

a   3:2 Literally "dogs," which is a figure of speech for religious hypocrites

b   3:5 This meant that he could trace his family line all the way back to Abraham. There is also an inference that Paul spoke Hebrew-Aramaic as his native tongue and did not adopt Greek customs.

c   3:5 The tribe of Benjamin was honored as the tribe most loyal to the house of David. *Benjamin* means "son of my right hand."

d   3:5 A Pharisee was known as a "separated one," who religiously followed all the laws of Judaism.

e   3:6 Or "the written Law."

forsaken them and I regard it all as nothing compared to the delight of experiencing Jesus Christ as my Lord! [8]To truly know him meant letting go of everything from my past and throwing all my boasting and all that I thought made me better than others on the garbage heap. It's all like a pile of manure to me now, so that I may be enriched in the reality of knowing Jesus Christ and embrace him as Lord in all of his greatness.

[9]My passion is to be consumed with him and not clinging to my own "righteousness" based in keeping the written Law. My "righteousness" will be his, based on the faithfulness of Jesus Christ—the very righteousness that comes from God. [10]And I continually long to know the wonders of Jesus more fully and to experience the overflowing power of his resurrection working in me. I will be one with him in his sufferings and I will be one with him in his death. [11]Only then will I be able to experience complete oneness with him in his resurrection from the realm of death.

[12]I admit that I haven't yet acquired the absolute fullness that I'm pursuing, but I run with passion into his abundance so that I may reach the purpose that Jesus Christ has called me to fulfill and wants me to discover. [13]I don't depend on my own strength to accomplish this;[a] however I do have one compelling focus: I forget all of the past as I fasten my heart to the future instead. [14]I run straight for the divine invitation of reaching the heavenly goal and gaining the victory-prize through the anointing of Jesus. [15]So let all who are fully mature have this same passion, and if anyone is not yet gripped by these desires,[b] God will reveal it to them. [16]And let us all advance together to reach this victory-prize, following one path with one passion.

---

a 3:13 This phrase is translated literally from the Aramaic. The Greek text states "I, myself, have not taken possession of it."

b 3:15 The Aramaic literally means "those who don't run this way, God will reveal it to them."

[17]My beloved friends, imitate my walk with God and follow all those who walk according to the way of life we modeled before you. [18]For there are many who live by different standards. As I've warned you many times (I weep as I write these words), they are enemies of the cross of the Anointed One and [19]doom awaits them. Their god has possessed them and made them mute.[a] Their boast is in their shameful lifestyles and their minds are in the dirt.[b]

[20]But we are a colony[c] of heaven on earth as we cling tightly to our Life-Giver, the Lord Jesus Christ, [21]who will transform our humble bodies[d] and transfigure us into the identical likeness of his glorified body. And using his matchless power, he continually subdues everything to himself.[e]

Four

——

[1]My dear and precious friends, whom I deeply love, you have truly become my glorious joy and crown of reward. Now arise[f] in the fullness of your union with our Lord.

[2]And I plead with Euodia and Syntyche to settle their disagreement and be restored with one mind in our Lord.[g] [3]I would like my dear

---

a 3:19 Translated from the Aramaic. The Greek states "their god is their belly," which is meaningless to the average English speaker.
b 3:19 Translated from the Aramaic. It literally means "their conscience is in the ground."
c 3:20 Or, "citizenship," or, "commonwealth."
d 3:21 Or, "the body of our humility."
e 3:21 Implied in the text. The Aramaic is "everyone is in submission to him."
f 4:1 The Aramaic word "arise" implies "resurrection." The Greek is "stand fast."
g 4:2 In every church there is often found conflict in relationships. Paul seeks to encourage these two dear women to resolve all their disagreements. Their names give us a clue. Euodia comes from a word that means "a fair journey." Syntyche comes from a word that can mean "an accident." Along our fair journey we may collide with another, but God always has grace

friend Syzygos[a] to help resolve this issue, for both women have diligently labored with me for the prize and helped in spreading the revelation of the gospel,[b] along with Clement[c] and the rest of my coworkers. All of their names are written in the Book of Life.

[4]Be cheerful with joyous celebration in every season of life. Let joy overflow, for you are united with the Anointed One! [5]Let gentleness[d] be seen in every relationship, for our Lord is ever near.[e]

[6]Don't be pulled in different directions or worried about a thing. Be saturated in prayer throughout each day, offering your faith-filled requests before God with overflowing gratitude. Tell him every detail of your life, [7]then God's wonderful peace that transcends human understanding, will make the answers known to you through Jesus Christ.[f] [8]So keep your thoughts continually fixed on all that is authentic and real, honorable and admirable, beautiful and respectful, pure and holy, merciful and kind. And fasten your thoughts on every glorious work of God,[g] praising him always. [9]Follow the example of all that we have imparted to you and the God of peace will be with you in all things.

[10]My heart overflows with joy when I think of how you showed your love to me by your financial support of my ministry. For even

---

for restoration.

a 4:3 It is believed that Syzygos was one of the pastors of the church at Philippi. His name means "burden-bearer." Some believe this verse could also be translated "I also request, dear burden bearer, to help these women..."

b 4:3 The Aramaic can also be translated "God's kingdom realm."

c 4:3 Clement was one of the men who led the church in Philippi. His name means "mild" or "merciful."

d 4:5 The Greek word means "fairness;" the Aramaic "humility."

e 4:5 Or "approaching."

f 4:7 As translated literally from the Aramaic. The Greek is "guard your heart and your mind in Christ Jesus."

g 4:8 The Aramaic literally means "acts of glorification."

though you have so little, you still continue to help me at every opportunity. [11]I'm not telling you this because I need money, for I have learned to be satisfied and undisturbed in any circumstance.[a] [12-13]I know what it means to lack,[b] and I know what it means to experience overwhelming abundance. For I'm trained in the secret of overcoming all things, whether in fullness or in hunger. And I find that the strength of Christ's explosive power infuses me to conquer every difficulty.[c]

[14]You've so graciously provided for my essential needs during this season of difficulty—in spite of all that you were going through.[d] [15]For I want you to know that the Philippian church was the only church that supported me in the beginning as I went out to preach the gospel as a missionary to Macedonia.[e] You were the only church that sowed into me financially,[f] [16]and when I was in Thessalonica, you supported me for well over a year.[g]

[17]I mention this not because I'm requesting a gift, but so that the fruit of your generosity may bring you an abundant reward. [18]I now have all I need—more than enough—I'm abundantly satisfied! For I've received the gift you sent by Epaphroditus and viewed it as a sweet sacrifice, perfumed with the fragrance of your faithfulness, which is so pleasing to God!

[19]I am convinced that my God will fully satisfy every need you have, for I have seen the abundant riches of glory revealed to me through the

---

a 4:11 Or "to give up everything I have."
b 4:12–13 Or "humbled."
c 4:12–13 Or "to master all things."
d 4:14 This last phrase is not in the Aramaic text, but is included in the Greek.
e 4:15 Implied in the text.
f 4:15 The Aramaic literally means "accounts of planting and giving."
g 4:16 As translated from the Aramaic. The Greek means "twice you sent gifts."

Anointed One, Jesus Christ! [20]And God our Father will receive all the glory and the honor throughout the eternity of eternities! Amen!

[21]Give my warm greetings to all the believers in the Anointed One, Jesus. [22]All the brothers and sisters in Christ that are here with me send their loving greetings, especially the converts from Caesar's household.

[23]May every one of you overflow with the grace and favor of our Lord Jesus Christ![a]

Love in Christ,
Paul

---

a 4:23 As translated from the Aramaic. The Greek states "with your spirit."

Colossians

HEAVEN'S HOPE

Translator's Introduction to Colossians

AT A GLANCE

Author: The apostle Paul

Audience: The church of Colossae

Date: AD 60–61

Type of Literature: A letter

Major Themes: Christ, the church, the gospel, and the Christian life.

Outline:

Letter Opening — 1:1–2:5
Letter Theme: Christ-Centered Living — 2:6–7
Threats to Christ-Centered Living — 2:8–23
Living a Christ-Centered Life — 3:1–4:6
Letter Closing — 4:7–18

ABOUT COLOSSIANS

What a glorious hope lives within us! This is the theme of Paul's masterpiece written to the church of Colossae—our hope of glory!

The beauty and revelation that comes into us when we receive the truth of this letter is astounding. The Holy Spirit hands to us many wonderful nuggets of gold here. The heavenly hope of glory, the mystery hidden and reserved for this generation, is Jesus our anointed Messiah.

Paul penned this letter while in a prison cell. When hope was absent in his environment, Paul rediscovered it in his enjoyment of Christ within himself. No matter where you live or what surrounds you in this moment, there is a burning hope inside your soul that does more than just carry you through—it releases the heavenly Christ within. Great comfort and encouragement can be found by reading the letter to the Colossians.

Written about AD 60, Paul seeks to focus on the wonderful hope of the gospel and reminds the believers to not turn aside or fall victim to those who would minimize Christ and lead the church into empty philosophies and humanism. Already, there were many false teachers and cults that were forming and deceiving new believers and drawing them away from the supremacy of Christ. Many have noted that of all Paul's letters, Colossians speaks more of the importance of Christ than any other.

Nearly everyone who has studied Colossians would agree that the summary of this letter can be found in 1:18–19:

He is the Head of his body, which is the church. And since he is the beginning and the firstborn heir in resurrection, he must always be embraced as the most exalted One, holding first place in everything. For God is satisfied to have all his perfection dwell in Christ.

We can never be moved away from our glorious Head, Jesus Christ! To see him is to see the fullness of the Father and the fullness of the Holy Spirit. How we love this Firstborn Heir of all things!

PURPOSE

The major reason why Paul wrote this letter was to equip the Colossian church to fend off false teaching and help them resist false teachers within the community. It seems as though certain Christians in the city had believed and were promoting a version of Christianity that threatened orthodox beliefs and practices that stood in contrast to what the Colossian church had received from Epaphras. Paul judged this version to not only be deficient but dangerous. He penned this letter to remind believers of the wonderful hope of the gospel and not to turn aside or fall victim to those who would minimize Christ and lead the church into empty philosophies and humanism.

AUTHOR AND AUDIENCE

Although the apostle Paul wrote this letter to the church of Colossae, we do not believe he was the one who started this church, nor had he ever been to the city. It was most likely the result of Paul's three-year ministry in Ephesus, which was less than a hundred miles away. So effective was Paul's preaching and teaching that his converts spread the message out of Ephesus throughout the region known as Asia Minor. Most likely it was Epaphras who was the church planter in the Lycus Valley, which included the cities of Laodicea, Hieropolis, and Colossae.

Although Paul had never visited their city, he had heard of the believers of Colossae and began to pray for them that they would advance and become the fullness of Christ on the earth. Perhaps the new converts had met first in the home of Philemon until they outgrew the "house church." How tenderly Paul speaks to them, as a father in the faith, to motivate them to keep their hearts and beliefs free from error. The church today needs to hear these truths.

MAJOR THEMES

The supremacy and centrality of Christ. The key theme to Paul's letter to the church at Colossae is the supremacy and centrality of Christ. One of the clearest pictures we have of this theme is the famed *Christ Hymn* of 1:15-20. Colossians makes it clear that in reigning supreme Jesus is himself God. As God he reigns over all creation. Paul also makes it clear that Jesus is all sufficient for our spiritual life, and should reign supreme at its center.

The body of Christ. One of the most unique aspects of this letter is Paul's description of the church as Christ's "body." He presents Christ as the church's ruler, who has authority over her and who also sustains her. And as Christ's body, we are the continuing presence of Christ on the earth; through the church the mission of Christ is revealed and advanced.

The true gospel. The major purpose for Paul's letter was to confront false teachers and their false gospel. Apparently, they were adding to the gospel Epaphras taught—mixing Jewish legalism, human tradition, and angel worship. Paul urges the Colossians to reject this religious enslavement and remember the true message of Christ and his lasting hope: "Never be shaken from the hope of the gospel you have believed in."

The Christian life. Using the metaphor of a body, Paul teaches that our life as Christians must be rooted in Christ—he is the Head, after all. He is the one who empowers us and renews us; we have our entire existence in him! Since it is through Christ we live as Christians, a "rules-oriented" lifestyle dictated by humans will not lead to spiritual growth.

———

I'm so thankful for Colossians. Translating this letter moved my heart into the sacred flame, and I know reading it will do the same for you, my friend. Get ready for some of the most glorious words you could ever read. They are inspired, anointed, loaded with life, and full of hope—for they point us to the one we love—Jesus Christ!

One

___

Dear friends in Colossae,

¹⁻²My name is Paul and I have been chosen by Jesus Christ to be his apostle, by the calling and destined purpose of God. My colleague, Timothy, and I send this letter to all the holy believers who have been united in Jesus as beloved followers of the Messiah. May God, our true Father, release upon your lives the riches of his kind favor and heavenly peace through the Lord Jesus, the Anointed One.

³⁻⁴Every time we pray for you our hearts overflow with thanksgiving to Father-God, the Father of our Lord Jesus Christ. For we have heard of your devoted lives of faith and the tender love you have for all his holy believers. And from the first time we heard about your conversion until now we faithfully prayed for you, ⁵that you would access your destiny through all the treasures of your inheritance stored up in the heavenly realm. For the revelation of the true gospel is as real today as the day you first heard of our glorious hope, now that you have believed in the the truth of the gospel.

⁶This is the wonderful message that is being spread everywhere, powerfully changing hearts throughout the earth, just like it has changed you! Every believer of this good news bears the fruit of eternal life as they experience the reality of God's grace.

[7]Our beloved coworker, Epaphras,[a] was there from the beginning to thoroughly teach you the astonishing revelation of the gospel. I can always depend on him, for he serves you faithfully as Christ's representative. [8]He's informed us of the many wonderful ways love is being demonstrated through your lives by the empowerment of the Holy Spirit.

[9]Since we first heard about you, we've kept you always in our prayers that you would receive the perfect knowledge of God's pleasure[b] over your lives, making you reservoirs of every kind of wisdom and spiritual understanding. [10]We pray that you would walk in the ways of true righteousness, pleasing God in every good thing you do. Then you'll become fruit-bearing branches, yielding to his life, and maturing in the rich experience of knowing God in his fullness! [11]And we pray that you would be energized with all his explosive power from the realm of his magnificent glory, filling you with great hope.[c]

[12]Your hearts can soar with joyful gratitude when you think of how God made you worthy to receive the glorious inheritance freely given to us. This is what every holy believer is qualified to experience by living in the light.[d] [13]He has rescued us completely from the tyrannical rule[e] of darkness and has translated us into the kingdom realm of his beloved Son. [14]For in the Son all our sins are canceled and we have the release of redemption through the ransom price he paid—his very blood.

[15]He is the divine portrait, the true likeness of the invisible God, and the firstborn Heir of all creation. [16]For through the Son everything

---

a 1:7 The church of Colossae was not planted by Paul but by Epaphras. His name means "lovely." He imparted to the church faith and love, praying always for them. See Col. 4:12.

b 1:9 Or "experience God's will for your lives." The Greek word *thelema*, can also mean "desire" or "pleasure."

c 1:11 As translated from the Aramaic. The Greek text means "patient endurance."

d 1:12 Or "by enlightening us."

e 1:13 Or "authority."

was created, both in the heavenly realm and on the earth, all that is seen and all that is unseen. Every seat of power, realm of government, principality, and authority—it was all created through him and for his purpose! [17]He existed before anything was made, so now everything finds completion in him.

[18]He is the Head of his body, which is the church. And since he is the Beginning and the Firstborn Heir in resurrection,[a] he must always be embraced as the most exalted One, holding first place[b] in everything. [19]For God is satisfied to have all his fullness[c] dwelling in Christ. [20]And by the blood of his cross, everything in heaven and earth is brought back to himself—back to its original intent, restored to innocence again![d]

[21-22]Even though you were once distant from him, living in the shadows of your evil thoughts and actions, he reconnected you back to himself. He released his supernatural peace to you through the sacrifice of his own body as the sin-payment on your behalf so that you would dwell in his presence. And now there is nothing between you and Father God, for he sees you as holy, flawless, and restored,[e] [23]if indeed you continue to advance in faith, assured of a firm foundation to grow upon. Never be shaken from the hope of the gospel[f] you have believed in. And this is the glorious news I preach all over the world.

[24]I can even celebrate the sorrows I have experienced on your behalf; for as I join with you in your difficulties, it helps you to discover

---

a 1:18 Implied in the text. Literally "from the dead."
b 1:18 In the Greek text this is a title, "the Holder of First Place" or "the Superior One."
c 1:19 This includes all the fullness of God, the fullness of his plan for our lives, and the full image of God being restored into our hearts.
d 1:20 Implied in the context. It literally means "back to himself." Some scholars believe that Colossians 1:15–20 is actually lyrics of an ancient hymn sung in the churches.
e 1:21–22 Or "without an indictment."
f 1:23 Or in the Aramaic "the revelation of the kingdom."

what lacks in your understanding[a] of the sufferings Jesus Christ experienced for his body, the church. [25]This is the very reason I've been made a minister by the authority of God and a servant to his body, so that in his detailed plan I would fully equip you with the Word of God.

[26]There is a divine mystery—a secret surprise that has been concealed from the world for generations, but now it's being revealed, unfolded and manifested for every holy believer to experience. [27]Living within you is the Christ who floods you with the expectation of glory! This mystery of Christ, embedded within us, becomes a heavenly treasure chest of hope filled with the riches of glory for his people, and God wants everyone to know it!

[28-29]Christ is our message! We preach to awaken hearts and bring every person into the full understanding of truth. It has become my inspiration and passion in ministry to labor with a tireless intensity, with his power flowing through me, to present to every believer the revelation of being his perfect one in Jesus Christ.

Two

[1]I wish you could know how much I have struggled[b] for you and for the church in Laodicea, and for the many other friends I've yet to meet. [2] I am contending for you that your hearts will be wrapped in the comfort

---

a 1:24 Implied in the context. The text contains an ellipsis that is completed by the translation. The sufferings of Christ were complete, sufficient to transfer righteousness and forgiveness to every believer. Paul's sufferings were meant to be an example of Christ and a testimony to his converts that his ministry was sincere.

b 2:1 The Greek word *agon* (from which we get "agony") means an intense conflict and struggle. This could imply Paul's apostolic intercession for them.

of heaven and woven together into love's fabric. The certainty of your faith will give you access[a] to all the riches of God as you experience the revelation of God's great mystery—Christ unveiled within you.[b]

³For our spiritual wealth is in him, like hidden treasure waiting to be discovered—heaven's wisdom and endless riches of revelation knowledge.

⁴I want you to know this so that no one will come and lead you into error[c] through their persuasive arguments and clever words. ⁵Even though I'm separated from you geographically, my spirit is present there with you. And I'm overjoyed to see how disciplined[d] and deeply committed you are because you have such a solid faith in Christ, the Anointed One.

⁶In the same way you received Jesus our Lord and Messiah by faith, continue your journey of faith, progressing further into your union with him! ⁷Your spiritual roots go deeply into his life as you are continually infused with strength, encouraged in every way. For you are established in the faith you have absorbed and enriched by your devotion to him![e]

⁸Beware that no one distracts you or intimidates you[f] in their attempt to lead you away from Christ's fullness by pretending to be full of wisdom when they're filled with endless arguments of human logic. For they operate with humanistic and clouded judgments based on the mindset of this world system, and not the anointed truths of the Anointed One.

⁹For he is the complete fullness of deity living in human form.

---

a   2:2 Or in the Aramaic "approach."
b   2:2 Implied in the context.
c   2:4 By implication, this "error" would be the teaching that Jesus is not enough, adding something to the all-sufficient Christ.
d   2:5 The Greek text literally means "unbroken battle formation." The Aramaic literally means "organized" or "principled."
e   2:7 As translated from the Aramaic. The Greek states "overflowing with gratitude."
f   2:8 The Aramaic literally means "strips you naked." The Greek states "takes you captive."

[10]And our own completeness is now found in him. We are completely filled with God as Christ's fullness overflows within us. He is the Head[a] of every kingdom and authority in the universe!

[11]Through our union with him we have experienced circumcision of heart. All of the guilt and power of sin[b] has been cut away and is now extinct. And it wasn't because of something good that we have done, but because of what Christ, the Anointed One, has accomplished for us.

[12]For we've been buried with him, immersed into his death. Our "baptism into death" also means we were raised with him when we believed in God's resurrection power, the power that raised him from death's realm. [13]This "realm of death" describes our former state, for we were held in sin's grasp.[c] But now, we've been resurrected out of that "realm of death" never to return, for we are forever alive and forgiven of all our sins!

[14]And through the divine authority of his cross, he canceled out every legal violation we had on our record and the old arrest warrant that stood to indict us. He erased it all—our sins, our stained[d] soul, and our shameful failure to keep his laws—he deleted it all and they cannot be retrieved! Everything we once were in Adam[e] has been placed onto his cross and nailed permanently there as a public display of cancellation.

[15]Then Jesus made a public spectacle of all the powers and

---

a   2:10 Or "Source."

b   2:11 The Aramaic literally means "flesh of sin." The Greek means "body of the natural realm."

c   2:13 Literally "the uncircumcision of your flesh."

d   2:14 This "stained soul" has been erased of its filth. The word "erased" explicitly holds the concept of removal of stains. This would mean the nature of Adam has been erased and the nature of Christ has been embedded into us. We are totally set free from every trace of sin by the power of the blood of Jesus Christ.

e   2:14 The Aramaic literally means "from our midst." This would refer to all that was within us—the core of our past life and its memories of failure and disobedience. A new DNA has been embedded now within us through the cross and resurrection life of Christ.

principalities of darkness, stripping away from them every weapon and all their spiritual authority and power[a] to accuse us. And by the power of the cross, Jesus led them around as prisoners in a procession of triumph. He was not their prisoner; they were his![b]

[16]Since you have been set free, why would you allow anyone[c] to judge you because of what you eat or drink, or insist that you keep the feasts, observe new moon celebrations, or the Sabbath? [17]All of these were but a prophetic shadow and the evidence of what would be fulfilled,[d] for the body[e] is now Christ!

[18]Don't let anyone disqualify you from your prize! Don't let their pretended sincerity fool you as they deliberately lead you into their initiation of angel worship.[f] For they take pleasure in pretending to be experts of something they know nothing about. Their reasoning is

---

a   2:15 Literally "governments and authorities."

b   2:15 Implied by the obvious irony in the Greek. The Aramaic text has a phrase that is not found in Greek manuscripts. The Aramaic is "having *put off his body,* he stripped principalities and powers and shamed them openly." This implies that between the day of crucifixion and the day of resurrection while in the spirit-realm, Jesus destroyed death, the powers of darkness, and every work of the enemy through the blood of his cross. All the enemy's weapons have been stripped away from him and now the church has authority in Christ to enforce this triumph upon the dethroned rulers of this world. However, an alternate translation of the Aramaic could be "after *sending out his body* [apostles, prophets, evangelists, pastors, teachers, believers], they enforced his triumph to all the thrones and authorities, putting them all to public shame by the manifestation of himself [in them]."

c   2:16 The Aramaic text implies "any unbeliever."

d   2:17 The revelation of the Old Testament is so rich when we understand that its shadow is displaced by the body of Christ, the full revelation of who he is. The shadow only reflects the substance of what has now been fulfilled.

e   2:17 Or "substance."

f   2:18 In the first century AD, there was a mystical Jewish religion called Merkabah Mysticism, or Chariot Mysticism, in which the initiate would seek to go into the palace of God through meditation and enter into his chariot-throne. His was the innermost palace of seven concentric heavenly palaces surrounding his chariot-throne. At each "palace" or level there would be a fierce protecting angel, acting as a mediator who had to be placated by angel worship, which would enable the worshiper to enter the next level. There were also ancient polytheistic folk religions that worshiped and invoked angels. These were entirely forbidden paths for believers in Jesus, and Paul warned them of that in this letter.

meaningless and comes only from their own opinions. [19]They refuse to take hold of the true source, and honor him as the Head.

But we receive directly from him, and his life supplies[a] vitality into every part of his body through the joining ligaments connecting us all as one. He is the divine Head who guides his body and causes it to grow by the supernatural power of God.[b]

[20]For you were included in the death of Christ and have died with him to the religious system and powers of this world. Don't retreat back to being bullied by the standards and opinions of religion—[21]for example, their strict requirements, "You can't associate with that person!" or, "Don't eat that!" or, "You can't touch that!" [22]These are the doctrines of men and corrupt customs that are worthless to help you spiritually. [23]For though they may appear to possess the promise of wisdom in their submission to God through the deprivation of their physical bodies, it is actually nothing more than empty rules rooted in religious rituals!

Three

[1]Christ's resurrection is your resurrection too. This is why we are to yearn for all that is above, for that's where Christ sits enthroned at the place of all power, honor, and authority![c] [2]Yes, feast on all the treasures

---

a   2:19 The Greek word used here is *epichoregeo*, which interestingly can be translated as "to lead the chorus," or "choir director." It was used to denote a person who paid for the expenses of a Greek drama, and who supplied all their needs throughout its production. Similarly, Jesus tunes us up to heaven's notes, and draws out of us the melody of his divine symphony. He supplies the music to us, and imparts the wisdom for us to play it under his direction. This is the artful picture of how Jesus orchestrates his body with its many members.

b   2:19 Or "makes it grow with the discipline from God."

c   3:1 The "right hand of God," is an obvious metaphor for the place of power, authority, honor,

of the heavenly realm and fill your thoughts with heavenly realities, and not with the distractions of the natural realm.

³Your crucifixion[a] with Christ has severed the tie to this life, and now your true life is hidden away in God as you live within the Anointed One. ⁴And as Christ himself is seen for who he really is, who you really are will also be revealed, for you are now one with him in his glory!

⁵So you must consider your life in this natural realm as already dead and buried. Live as one who has died to every form of sexual sin and impurity. Live as one who died to diseases,[b] and desires for forbidden things,[c] including the desire for wealth, which is the essence of idol worship. ⁶When you live in these vices you ignite the anger of God against these acts of disobedience.[d]

⁷⁻⁸That's how you behaved before you were joined to Christ. You once were characterized by your evil deeds, but now it's time to eliminate them from your lives once and for all—anger, fits of rage, all forms of hatred,[e] cursing,[f] filthy speech, ⁹and lying.[g] Now that you have embraced new creation life as the true reality, lay aside[h] your old Adam-self with its masquerade and disguise.

¹⁰For you have acquired new creation life which is continually being renewed into the likeness of the One who created you; giving

---

and glory.

a 3:3 The Aramaic could be translated "Your death and your life are both hidden with the Messiah in God."

b 3:5 This is only found in the Aramaic manuscripts. It is omitted in the Greek.

c 3:5 The Aramaic word implies "magic."

d 3:6 As translated from the Aramaic. The Greek states "the sons of disobedience," but it is actually the "deeds" which are punished as seen in verses 7–9. The Aramaic word used here is a homonym that can mean either "sons" or "deeds," which may explain the variation within Greek manuscripts.

e 3:7–8 Including self-hatred.

f 3:7–8 As translated from the Aramaic. The Greek means "slander."

g 3:9 Or "living a lie."

h 3:9 As translated from the Greek. The Aramaic has a command, "take off the old life."

you the full revelation of God. [11]In this new creation life, your nationality makes no difference, or your ethnicity, education, or economic status—they matter nothing. For it is Christ that means everything as he lives in every one of us![a]

[12]You are always and dearly loved by God! So robe yourself with virtues of God, since you have been divinely chosen to be holy. Be merciful as you endeavor to understand others, and be compassionate, showing kindness toward all. Be gentle and humble, unoffendable in your patience with others. [13]Tolerate the weaknesses of those in the family of faith, forgiving one another in the same way you have been graciously forgiven by Jesus Christ. If you find fault with someone, release this same gift of forgiveness to them. [14]For love is supreme and must flow through each of these virtues. Love becomes the mark[b] of true maturity.[c]

[15]Let your heart be always guided[d] by the peace of the Anointed One, who called you to peace as part of his one body. And always be thankful, overflowing with gratitude for your life-union with Christ.

[16]Let the word of Christ live[e] in you richly, flooding you with all wisdom. Apply the Scriptures as you teach and instruct one another with the Psalms, and with festive praises,[f] and with prophetic songs given to you spontaneously by the Spirit. As the fountain of grace overflows within you, sing to God with all your hearts!

---

a   3:11 Or "there is neither Jew or Scythians, circumcision or uncircumcision, neither Greek nor barbarian, neither slave nor free, but the Messiah is all and in all."
b   3:14 The Aramaic means "the girdle of maturity."
c   3:14 Or "perfection."
d   3:15 The Greek literally means "let peace be the umpire of your minds."
e   3:16 Or "grow."
f   3:16 Or "hymns."

[17]Let every activity[a] of your lives and every word[b] that comes from your lips be drenched with the beauty of our Lord Jesus, the Anointed One. And bring your constant praise to God the Father because of what Christ has done for you!

[18]Let every wife be supportive and tenderly devoted[c] to her husband, for this is a beautiful illustration[d] of our devotion to Christ. [19]Let every husband be filled with cherishing love for his wife and never be insensitive[e] toward her.

[20]Let the children respect and pay attention to their parents in everything for this pleases our Lord Jesus. [21]And fathers, don't have unrealistic expectations[f] for your children or else they may become discouraged.

[22]Let every employee listen well and follow the instructions of their employer, not just when their employers are watching, and not in pretense, but faithful in all things. For we are to live our lives with pure hearts in the constant awe and wonder of our Lord God.

[23]Put your heart and soul into every activity you do, as though you are doing it for the Lord himself and not merely for others.

[24]For we know that we will receive a reward, an inheritance of kingdom authority[g] from the Lord, as we serve the Lord Yahweh,[h] the

---

a 3:17 The Aramaic is "commitment."

b 3:17 The Aramaic is "oath."

c 3:18 The Greek word, *hupotasso*, can be translated "submitted," "attached," or "supportive." The Aramaic word is best translated as "tenderly devoted." Both concepts are included in this translation.

d 3:18 Implied in the text.

e 3:19 Or bitter."

f 3:21 Or "exasperate your children."

g 3:24 Implied in the text.

h 3:24 Although absent in the Greek manuscripts, the Aramaic text makes it abundantly clear that it is Jesus Christ who is the Lord God (Yahweh). See also Luke 2:11 TPT.

Anointed One! [25]A disciple will be repaid for what he has learned and followed,[a] for God pays no attention to the titles or prestige of men.

Four

———

[1]Employers, treat your workers with equality and justice as you know that you also have a Lord and Master in heaven who is watching you.[b]

[2]Be faithful to pray as intercessors who are fully alert and giving thanks to God. [3]And please pray for me, that God will open a door of opportunity for us to preach the revelation of the mystery of Christ, for whose sake I am imprisoned. [4]Pray that I would unfold and reveal fully this mystery, for that is my delightful assignment.

[5]Walk in the wisdom of God as you live before the unbelievers,[c] and make it your duty[d] to make him known. [6]Let every word you speak be drenched with grace[e] and tempered with truth and clarity.[f] For then you will be prepared to give a respectful answer to anyone who asks about your faith.

[7-8]Now let me tell you about what is happening with me. I have sent Tychicus to you so that he could find out how you are doing in

---

a 3:25 This clause is translated literally from the Aramaic. The Greek text reads "He who does wrong will receive the consequences for what he has done."
b 4:1 Implied in the text.
c 4:5 The Aramaic could be translated "as you live in the wilderness."
d 4:5 The Aramaic literally means "sell your last crust of bread," which is a metaphor for making a full commitment (i.e. giving all you've got).
e 4:6 The Aramaic word could also be translated "compassion."
f 4:6 Literally "seasoned with salt." This is an idiom that means "friendly, clear, and making people thirsty for truth."

your journey of faith,[a] and bring comfort and encouragement to your hearts. He comes with my recommendation, for he is a beloved brother in Christ, a faithful servant of the gospel and my ministry partner in our Master Yahweh's[b] work.

[9]I have also sent Onesimus,[c] who is from your city,[d] to return to you. He also is a beloved and faithful brother who will inform you of all that we're enduring in Rome.[e]

[10-11]Aristarchus, a fellow prisoner here with me, sends you his love. And Joshua (who is also called Justus) along with Mark, the cousin of Barnabas, also send you their loving greetings. You have already been informed that if Mark comes to you, receive him warmly in Christ. These three men are the only Jewish converts to Christ who have aided me here in the work of the kingdom of God, and they have been a great blessing to me.

[12-13]Epaphras, who is also from Colossae, sends his loving greetings. I can tell you that he is a true servant of Christ, who always labors and intercedes for you. His prayers are filled with requests to God that you would grow and mature, standing complete and perfect in the beauty of God's plan for your lives. Epaphras has such great zeal and passion for you and for those who are from Laodicea and from Hierapolis.

[14]And Luke, the beloved physician, sends his warm greetings to you, and Demas also. [15]Continue to pray for the peace and blessing of

---

a 4:7-8 Or "that I may know your affairs."

b 4:7-8 Again, the Aramaic title for Jesus is Lord (Master) Yahweh; this is the clearest title that could be stated to prove the deity of Jesus Christ.

c 4:9 This was the slave who ran away from his master, Philemon, who was a friend to the Apostle Paul. See Philemon 1:10-12

d 4:9 Or "he is one of you."

e 4:9 Implied in the context.

the believers in Laodicea. And pray for dear Nymphas and the church that gathers in her[a] home.

[16]Once you've read this letter publicly to the church, please send it on to the church of the Laodiceans,[b] and make sure you read the letter that I wrote to them. [17]Be sure you give Archippus this message: "Be faithful to complete the ministry you received from our Lord Jesus and don't give in to your problems until they yield the victory God intends for you to have!"[c]

[18]Now finally, I, Paul, write this with my own handwriting, and I send my loving greetings to you! Remember me in my imprisonment. May the blessings of God's grace overwhelm you!

Love in Christ,
Paul

---

a 4:15 There is some debate about the gender of Nymphas. It may be that many of those who translated this in the early church had difficulty with a church being led by a woman. There are some manuscripts in Greek that have "the church that meets in *her* house."

b 4:16 As stated in the introduction to Ephesians, it is most likely that this missing letter to the Laodiceans is, in fact, the letter to the Ephesian church. However, the tradition of the Eastern Church is that the letter to the Laodiceans was actually 1 and 2 Thessalonians.

c 4:17 It is believed that Archippus was a spiritual leader in the region of Colossae, perhaps the bishop of Laodicea; he is also mentioned in Philemon 2. We can only speculate why Paul wanted this exhortation to be made to him. Some believe he was a minister of Christ who was discouraged and needed to be exhorted to not abandon his calling.

1 Timothy

HEAVEN'S TRUTH

Translator's Introduction to 1 Timothy

AT A GLANCE

Author: The apostle Paul

Audience: Timothy, Paul's spiritual son in the faith

Date: AD 62–63

Type of Literature: A letter

Major Themes: False teachers, false doctrine, church leadership, and God's household.

Outline:

Letter Opening — 1:1–2
Ordering and Organizing the Church, Part 1 — 1:3–3:16
Ordering and Organizing the Church, Part 2 — 4:1–6:19
Letter Closing — 6:20–21

ABOUT 1 TIMOTHY

1 and 2 Timothy have been recognized as "Pastoral Epistles"—letters written by Paul for pastors and leaders to help them bring order and ordain elders (pastors) for the churches he planted. In fact, Timothy was an apostolic apprentice to Paul, mentored by a spiritual father who

poured into his life, even after being sent out to establish churches and bring them to maturity. Timothy was the extension of Paul's apostolic ministry. Perhaps we should view these two letters more as "Apostolic Epistles" instead of Pastoral Epistles.

One reason we know that Timothy's ministry was unlike the pastoral ministry of today is that Timothy was an itinerant apostle who planted and brought healing and truth to the churches in which he ministered. Some of the locations he ministered in would include Thessalonica (1 Thessalonians 3:2–6), Corinth (1 Corinthians 4:17; 16:10; 2 Corinthians 1:19), Philippi (Philippians 2:19–23), Berea (Acts 17:14), and Ephesus (1 Timothy 1:2). His ministry eventually brought him imprisonment, much like his apostolic mentor, Paul (Hebrews 13:23).

Timothy's name means "honored by God." He was from the city of Lystra, the place where Paul was stoned to death and then raised from the dead. It may have been that Timothy witnessed what happened to Paul and was converted through what he saw. Paul recruited young Timothy and raised him up to take the message of the gospel to the nations. He soon began to travel with Paul in his missionary journeys and was eventually trusted with great responsibilities to teach and instruct the church.

Timothy was the son of a mixed marriage with a Greek father and a Jewish mother, whose name was Eunice ("joyous victory"). His mother was a convert to Christ and was distinguished by her faith. Timothy was likely in his thirties when Paul wrote him this challenging letter.

Timothy's ministry was in more than one location, for he was told to do the "work of an evangelist" in planting churches and winning souls to Christ. He was Paul's faithful representative to the churches of Thessalonica (1 Thessalonians 3:2), Corinth (1 Corinthians 4:17), Philippi (Philippians 2:19), and Ephesus (1 Timothy 1:3)—yet it was in Ephesus where Paul left him to keep watering the seeds that had been planted to help the church there mature.

Paul instructs Timothy about the administration of the church and encourages him to hold up a high standard for those who lead. The qualifications for church leadership are spelled out in 1 Timothy (and Titus). And we are given clear instructions about caring for widows and for supporting the leaders of the church financially. Generally speaking, 1 Timothy could be seen as a manual for church planting. The key verse is found in 3:15:

But if I'm delayed in coming, you'll already have these instructions on how to conduct the affairs of the church of the living God, his very household, the supporting pillar and firm foundation of the truth.

What heavenly principles are revealed in this letter!

PURPOSE

The clear purpose of 1 Timothy is to reveal and emphasize the glorious truths of God. False teachers had begun to infiltrate the church of Ephesus, and Timothy was given the mission of preserving the truth and cleansing the church of error. Good relationships and spiritual growth can only come when the church grows in maturity and knows the difference between truth and error. There are wonderful revelations waiting for us in 1 Timothy that will focus our hearts on Christ, his glory, and his resurrection.

AUTHOR AND AUDIENCE

What beautiful words Paul shares with his spiritual son, Timothy! We are about to overhear the intimate words of encouragement and inspiration that a first-century apostle shared with his protégé. If we have any example at all of mentoring in the Bible, it is seen here in the relationship Paul had with Timothy. Written about AD 62–63, Paul imparts to Timothy the wisdom and revelation that is required to plant churches and lead an entire region into spiritual breakthrough.

MAJOR THEMES

False teachers and doctrine. Every generation has seen its fair share of false teaching; ours is no different, and neither was Timothy's. Paul commands him to confront false teachers and oppose unorthodox doctrines that "emphasize nothing more than the empty words of men." He exhorts him to maintain his personal faith and warns against falling away, like others.

Qualifications for church leaders. In this letter to his ministry coworker, Paul has provided the church throughout the ages a helpful list of qualifications for two offices: overseers/elders and deacons. Both church officers are called to a similar standard of high moral and personal conduct, which includes integrity, peace, temperateness, generosity, and a well-managed household.

The household of God. Throughout this letter from heaven, Paul explains what it means to live in the household of God. He outlines the proper treatment for widows, and he lays out the expectations for slaves, which can apply to workers too. He even says how the church should disciple its own. Paul gives Timothy the task of teaching Christ's vision for how his household should exist in the world.

———

Read 1 Timothy with a hungry heart, wrap it around your life, and watch God bring true growth and maturity into your spirit. I present to you Paul's first letter to Timothy!

One
___

To my dear son, Timothy,

[1]I'm writing to you as your apostolic father in Christ, for it was Jesus himself, our living Hope, who sent me as his servant by the command of God, our Life-Giver.[a]

[2]You are like a son to me, Timothy, my true spiritual son in the faith. May abundant grace, mercy, and total well-being[b] from God the Father and the Anointed One, our Lord Jesus, be yours!

[3]As I leave for Macedonia,[c] I'm asking that you remain in Ephesus and continue the discipleship of the believers; stay there in Ephesus and instruct them not to teach or follow the error of deceptive doctrines, [4]nor pay any attention to cultural myths, traditions, or the endless study of genealogies.[d] Those digressions only breed controversies and debates. They are devoid of power that builds up and strengthens the church in the faith of God.

[5]For we reach the goal of fulfilling all the commandments when we love others deeply with a pure heart, a clean conscience, and sincere faith. [6]Some believers have been led astray by teachings and speculations that emphasize nothing more than the empty words of men. [7]They presume to be expert teachers of the Law,[e] but they don't

___

a 1:1 Or "Savior."
b 1:2 The Hebrew concept of peace includes health, prosperity, and peace of mind.
c 1:3 As translated from the Aramaic.
d 1:4 The Jewish people have always been diligent to carefully record their genealogies; yet, the reference to genealogies here may also include the apocryphal writings of Jewish mysticism, detailing the origins of angelic beings involved in creation.
e 1:7 Or "Torah."

have the slightest idea of what they're talking about. They are dogmatic about peripheral issues and they simply love to argue!

⁸We know that the moral code of the Law is beautiful when applied as God intended, ⁹but actually, the Law was not established for righteous people, but to bring conviction of sin to the unrighteous. The Law was established to bring the revelation of sin to the evildoers and rebellious, the sinners without God, those who are vicious and perverse, and to those who strike their father or their mother.ᵃ

The Law will identify them as sinners—murderers, ¹⁰rapists, those who are sexually impure, homosexuals,ᵇ kidnappers, liars, those who break their oaths, and all those who oppose the teaching of godliness and purity in the church! They are the ones the Law is for.

¹¹I have been commissioned to preach the wonderful news of the glory of the exalted God. ¹²My heart spills over with thanks to God for the way he continually empowers me, and to our Lord Jesus, the Anointed One, who found me trustworthy and who authorized me to be his partner in this ministry.

¹³Mercy kissed me, even though I used to be a blasphemer, a persecutor of believers, and a scorner of what turned out to be true. God knew that I was ignorant and didn't know what I was doing. ¹⁴I was flooded with such incredible grace, *like a river overflowing its banks,*ᶜ until I was full of faith and love for Jesus, the Anointed One!

¹⁵I can testify that the Word is true and deserves to be received by all, for Jesus Christ came into the world to bring sinners back to life—even me, the worst sinner of all! ¹⁶Yet I was captured by grace,

---

a 1:9 As translated from the Aramaic. The Greek reads "those who murder their father or murder their mother."

b 1:10 Or in the Aramaic, "molesters of male children."

c 1:14 Paul uses the Greek word *pleonazō*, which means "super-abounding grace."

so that Jesus Christ could display through me the outpouring of his Spirit[a] as a pattern to be seen for all those who would believe[b] in him for eternal life.

[17]Because of this my praises rise to the King of all the universe[c] who is indestructible,[d] invisible, and full of glory, the only God[e] who is worthy of the highest honors throughout all of time and throughout the eternity of eternities! Amen!

[18-19]So Timothy, my son, I am entrusting you with this responsibility, in keeping with the very first prophecies that were spoken over your life, and are now in the process of fulfillment in this great work of ministry. Continue to use your prophecies as weapons as you wage spiritual warfare by faith and with a clean conscience. For there are many who reject these virtues and are now destitute of the true faith, [20]such as Hymenaeus[f] and Alexander[g] who have fallen away. I have delivered them both over to Satan to be rid of them and to teach them to no longer blaspheme!

---

a 1:16 As translated literally from the Aramaic. The Greek text reads "that Jesus would demonstrate his perfect patience."

b 1:16 Or "destined to believe."

c 1:17 Or "King of the Ages."

d 1:17 The Aramaic word used here is a direct reference to the physical body of Christ that did not decompose in the tomb, but was raised in resurrection.

e 1:17 As translated from the Aramaic. Some Greek texts have "the only wise God."

f 1:20 The name Hymenaeus is also the name of the pagan god of the bridal song sung by the attendants of the bride during the ceremony. He was invoked by the bride's friends in hope that he would come and manifest himself. Perhaps Hymenaeus was attempting to mix the worship of false gods into the church. See also 2 Timothy 2:17.

g 1:20 Alexander's name means "protector of men," or "man pleaser." When the church attempts to please men, we can quickly fail to please God.

Two

———

¹Most of all, I'm writing to encourage you to pray with gratitude to God. Pray for all men with all forms of prayers and requests as you intercede with intense passion. ²And pray for every political leader[a] and representative,[b] so that we would be able to live tranquil, undisturbed lives, free from persecution[c] as we worship the awe-inspiring God with pure hearts. ³It is pleasing to our Savior God to pray for them. ⁴He longs for everyone to embrace his life and return to the full knowledge of the truth.

⁵For God is one, and there is one Mediator between God and the sons of men—the true man, Jesus, the Anointed One. ⁶He gave himself as ransom-payment for everyone. Now is the proper time for God to give the world this witness. ⁷I have been divinely called as an apostle to preach this revelation, which is the truth. God has called me to be a trustworthy teacher to the nations, bringing people to faith in Christ.

⁸Therefore, I encourage the men to pray on every occasion[d] with hands lifted to God in worship with clean hearts, free from frustration or strife.[e] ⁹And that the women would also pray[f] with clean hearts, dressed appropriately and adorned modestly and sensibly, not flaunting

---

a   2:2 Or "kings."
b   2:2 Or "magistrates."
c   2:2 Implied in the text.
d   2:8 Or "wherever you pray."
e   2:8 Or "anger or scheming."
f   2:9 Prayer is implied, but made explicit from the context of verse 8.

their wealth.[a] [10]But they should be recognized instead by their beautiful deeds of kindness, suitable as one who worships God, living in awe of him.

[11]Let the women *who are new converts*[b] be willing to learn with all submission to their leaders and not speak out of turn.[c] [12]I don't advocate that the *newly converted*[d] women be the teachers in the church, assuming authority over the men, but to live in peace. [13]For God formed Adam first,[e] then Eve. [14]Adam did not mislead Eve, but Eve misled him and violated the command of God.[f] [15]Yet a woman shall live in restored dignity by means of her children, receiving the blessing that comes from raising them as consecrated children nurtured in faith and love, walking in wisdom.[g]

---

a 2:9 Literally "not with braids of gold, or with pearls, or gorgeous robes."

b 2:11 Implied and understood by the cultural context of that day.

c 2:11 Literally "quietly." In the context of that day, it referred to women arguing with their male congregational leaders. In the temple worship of Diana, the goddess of the Ephesian people, it was most common to have female leadership. For the women who converted to Christ, their only cultural context of worship was that the women were the leaders. In the church, however, it was the men who more commonly made up the leadership of the congregations. Paul telling the women to "learn in silence" means he was instructing them to take a respectful posture of a disciple in this new way of worshiping the true God. When Paul instructs them not to be teachers, he was apparently referring to their old religious system where it was the women who were the temple leaders and teachers of their goddess religion in Ephesus. This entire passage from 1 Timothy 2:9–15 is arguably one of the more difficult texts to translate in Paul's writings, and has a number of plausible translations and interpretations. However, the translator has chosen to make clear what was implicitly understood by the early Christians in Ephesus, making it explicit for those of us from another culture and another era.

d 2:12 Implied and understood by the cultural context of that day.

e 2:13 One of the prevailing Gnostic heresies of that era was that Eve was formed first, then Adam. Paul puts that debate to rest with this verse.

f 2:14 As translated from the Aramaic. The Greek says "Adam was not deceived but the woman was beguiled and has come into transgression."

g 2:15 As translated from the Aramaic. The Greek is "she shall be saved by childbearing," which could be misleading. The Aramaic makes it clear that the woman is honored and restored to dignity by her children (and spiritual children) who have faith in Christ, serving God. Some have interpreted the Greek text to imply that it was Mary who gave birth to Jesus and that he is the Child that saves us all and redeems womanhood.

Three

———

[1]If any of you[a] aspires to be an overseer[b] in the church; you have set your heart toward a noble ambition, for the Word is true! [2]Yet an elder needs to meet certain qualifications.

For example, an elder should be one who is without blame before others. He should be one whose heart is for his wife alone and not another woman.[c] He should be recognized as one who is sensible, and well-behaved, and living a disciplined life. He should be a "spiritual shepherd" who has the gift of teaching,[d] and is known for his hospitality.

[3]He cannot be a drunkard, or someone who lashes out at others,[e] or argumentative, or someone who simply craves more money,[f] but instead look for one who is peaceable, recognized by his gentleness.

[4]His heart should be set on guiding his household with wisdom and dignity;[g] bringing up his children to worship with devotion and purity. [5]For if he's unable to properly lead his own household well, how could he properly lead God's household?

---

a 3:1 Some translations have "men," however, the Greek word is not gender specific.

b 3:1 There are a number of terms that are synonymous for elder, such as: pastor, shepherd, presbyter, bishop, overseer, or guardian. These all describe the one office of pastor mentioned in Ephesians 4:11.

c 3:2 This literally means "a one woman kind of man" or "faithful to your woman [wife]," which implies much more than simply not being a polygamist. It was culturally common for men to have more than one wife or concubines in that era.

d 3:2 Or "able to teach."

e 3:3 The Aramaic literally means "not swift to strike."

f 3:3 The Aramaic literally means "merciful to money." Some see in this the concept of not showing favoritism because of someone's economic status.

g 3:4 Literally "beautifully."

⁶He should not be a new disciple[a] who would be vulnerable to living in the clouds of conceit and fall into pride, making him easy prey for Satan.[b] ⁷He should be respected by those who are unbelievers, having a beautiful testimony among them[c] so that he will not fall into the traps of Satan and be disgraced.

⁸And in the same way the deacons of the church[d] must be those who are pure and true to their word, not addicted to wine, or with greedy eyes on the contributions.[e] ⁹Instead, they must faithfully embrace the mysteries of faith while keeping a clean conscience. ¹⁰And each of them must be found trustworthy according to these standards before they are given the responsibility to minister as servant-leaders without blame.

¹¹And the women[f] also who serve the church should be dignified,[g] faithful in all things,[h] having their thoughts set on truth, and not known as those who gossip.

¹²A deacon's heart must be toward his wife alone and not another, leading his children and household with excellence. ¹³For those who serve in this way will obtain an honorable reputation[i] for themselves and a greater right to speak boldly in the faith that comes from the anointing of Jesus!

---

a 3:6 The Aramaic literally means "a new plant," which implies shallow roots.
b 3:6 The Greek literally means "fall into Satan's court of law."
c 3:7 As translated from the Greek. The literal Aramaic uses a metaphor: "a beautiful testimony from the wilderness." This means he has passed through his wilderness journey and is now seen as tested and proven.
d 3:8 Or in the Aramaic "ministers."
e 3:8 Or "corrupt profits."
f 3:11 The word used here can mean "women" or "wives." This may refer to women deacons. Phoebe is called a deacon in Romans 16:1.
g 3:11 As translated from the Greek, the Aramaic says "modest."
h 3:11 Or "temperate."
i 3:13 Or "a good rank."

¹⁴I'm writing all this with the expectation of seeing you soon. ¹⁵But if I'm delayed in coming, you'll already have these instructions on how to conduct the affairs of the church of the Living God, his very household and the supporting pillar and firm foundation of the truth.

¹⁶For the mystery of righteousness is truly amazing!

**He was revealed as a human being,
and as our great High Priest in the Spirit!ᵃ
Angels gazed upon him as a manᵇ
and the glorious message of his kingly rulership
is being preached to the nations!
Many have believed in him
and he has been taken back to heaven,
and has ascended into the place of exalted glory
in the heavenly realm.
Yes, great is this mystery of righteousness!**

---

a 3:16 As translated by the implication of the Aramaic. The Greek says "justified in the Spirit." Although some interpret it to mean his resurrection, that seems indefinite and with little meaning to today's reader. There is deep and beautiful poetic artistry here in this passage. The word order of the Aramaic lines is convincing that glorious and hidden truths are tucked into these verses; they are full of Jewish word plays and symbolism, and read like a poem. Many have concluded that this passage was an ancient hymn sung by the early church. Two different Aramaic words for "righteousness" are used in verse 16. The first word is *kanota* which is clearly connected to the word for "priest" or *kahna*. An Aramaic or Hebrew reader would clearly connect this "righteousness" to the priestly ministry. In poetic and perhaps subtle linguistic form, this points us to the High Priest of our faith. The second word used that is most often translated "righteousness" is *atzaddaq;* the word in the line before used for messenger (angels) is *malaka,* which is a form of the word for king (*malak*). To summarize, you have the words great (high), priest, king, and righteousness, which is the name for Melchizedek, (King of Righteousness). Truly, this mystery of righteousness is great!

b 3:16 Implied in the text. Some interpret this to refer to his ascension.

Four

___

¹The Holy Spirit has explicitly revealed:ᵃ At the end of this age, many will depart from the true faith one after another, devoting themselves to spiritsᵇ of deception and following demon-inspired revelations and theories. ²Hypocritical liarsᶜ will deceive many, for no matter what evil they do, their consciences won't bother them at all! ³And part of their deception will be in requiring celibacy and dietary restrictions that God doesn't expect, for he created all foods to be received with the celebration of faith by those who fully know the truth. ⁴We know that all creation is beautiful to God and there is nothing to be refused if it is received with gratitude. ⁵All that we eat is made sacred by the Word of God and prayer.

⁶If you will teach the believers these things, you will be known as a faithful and good minister of Jesus, the Anointed One. Nurture others in the living words of faith and in the knowledge of grace which you were taught.

⁷Be quick to abstain from senseless traditionsᵈ and legends,ᵉ but instead be engaged in the training of truth that brings righteousness.

⁸For athletic training only benefits you for a short season, but righteousness brings lasting benefit in everything; for righteousness

___

a 4:1 The Greek text could be translated "the Spirit says publicly." This is most likely through prophetic utterance in the church. God's Spirit still speaks to his people today through gifts of prophecy, tongues and interpretation of tongues, and in many other forms. Paul is likely quoting a prophecy.

b 4:1 Aramaic and Hebrew speakers would view this as an idiom for "deceiving prophecies."

c 4:2 The Aramaic literally means "they will seduce with false appearances."

d 4:7 Or "fables."

e 4:7 Or "the fiction of old wives' tales."

contains the promise of life, for time and eternity. [9]Faithful is the Word, and everyone should accept him![a]

[10]For the sake of this ministry, we toil tirelessly and are criticized continually,[b] simply because our hope is in the Living God. He is the wonderful Life-Giver[c] of all the children of men, and even more so to those who believe.

[11]Instruct and teach the people all that I've taught you. [12]And don't be intimidated by those who are older than you; simply be the example they need to see by being faithful and true in all that you do. Speak the truth[d] and live a life of purity and authentic love as you remain strong in your faith.

[13]So until I come, be diligent in devouring the Word of God, be faithful in prayer, and in teaching the believers.

[14]Don't minimize the powerful gift that operates in your life, for it was imparted to you by the laying on of hands of the elders and was activated through the prophecy they spoke over you. [15]Make all of this your constant meditation and make it real with your life so everyone can see that you are moving forward. [16]Give careful attention to your spiritual life and every cherished truth you teach, for living what you preach will then release even more abundant life inside you and to all those who listen to you.

---

a 4:9 As translated literally from the Aramaic. The Greek text reads "this is a faithful saying and is worthy to be fully accepted."

b 4:10 As translated from the Aramaic. In place of "criticized continually" the Greek text has "contend for the (athletic) prize."

c 4:10 As translated from the Aramaic. The Greek word is "Savior."

d 4:12 As translated from the Greek. The Aramaic could be translated "be an example through the Manifestation (Word)."

Five

¹Don't be harsh or verbally abusive to an older man;[a] it is better to appeal to him as a father. And as you minister to the younger men it is best to encourage them as your dear brothers. ²Honor the older women[b] as mothers, and the younger women, treat as your dear sisters with utmost purity.[c]

³The church needs to honor and support the widows, especially those who are in dire need. ⁴But if they have children or grandchildren at home, then it is only proper to let them provide for the ones who raised them when they were children, for kindness begins at home and it pleases God.

⁵For the true widow[d] is all alone and has placed her complete hope in God. She is Messiah's missionary[e] and will need the support of the church as one who remains in prayer day and night. ⁶But the widow who serves only herself lives a life of self-indulgence and is wasting her life away.

⁷Be sure to give clear instruction concerning these matters so that none of them will live with shame. ⁸For if a believer fails to provide for their own relatives when they are in need, they have compromised[f]

---

a   5:1 Or "elder" (one who is given responsibility within the church).
b   5:2 Or "woman elders."
c   5:2 Or "holiness."
d   5:5 There is an implication in the Aramaic that the "true widow" is one whose husband was killed due to persecution of believers.
e   5:5 As translated from the Aramaic.
f   5:8 Or "denied.

their convictions of faith and need to be corrected, for they are living worse than the unbelievers.

[9]The widows who are worthy to be supported by the church should be at least sixty years old and not remarried. [10]They should have a beautiful testimony of raising their families, practicing hospitality, encouraging other believers, comforting troubled ones,[a] and have a reputation for doing good works.

[11]But you need not concern yourself with the younger widows, for some will depart from the Messiah because of their desire to remarry.[b] [12]For they will face their own punishment[c] of living with a disturbed conscience for invalidating their former faith. [13]Those widows who go around from house to house as busybodies,[d] are only learning to be lazy, making their situation even worse by talking too much, gossiping, and speaking things they shouldn't. They become far too obsessed with empty things that will not bear good fruit.

[14]For this reason, teach the younger women to remarry and bear children and care for their household. This will keep them from giving our adversary a reason to gloat. [15]For there are already those who have begun to turn aside from their faith and are influenced by Satan.

[16]So if any believer has a widow in their family, instruct them to support her financially so that the church will not be burdened with her care. This will leave finances available for those widows who are truly in need.

[17]The pastors[e] who lead the church well should be paid well. They should receive double honor for faithfully preaching and teaching the

---

a   5:10 Or "paying the expenses of those who are persecuted."
b   5:11 There is a sexual connotation implied in the text.
c   5:12 Or "judgment."
d   5:13 The Greek word used for "busybodies" can also imply "gaining illegal knowledge of the supernatural." See Acts 19:19 where the same Greek word is used for black magic.
e   5:17 Or "elders." Also v. 19.

revelation of the Word of God. [18]For the Scriptures have taught us: "Do not muzzle an ox or forbid it to eat while it grinds the grain."[a] And also, "The one who labors deserves his wages."[b]

[19]Refuse to listen to suspicious accusations against the pastors who lead the flock unless you have two or three witnesses to confirm the accusations. [20]But if indeed you find that they have sinned, bring correction to them before the congregation so that the rest of the people will respect you.[c]

[21]Timothy, in the presence of God and our Lord Jesus Christ, and before the chosen messengers,[d] I solemnly charge you to put into practice all these matters without bias, prejudice, or favoritism.

[22]Don't be hasty to ordain them with the laying on of hands before you have discerned them properly, or you may end up sharing in their guilt should they fall. Keep yourself pure and holy with your standards high. [23][If drinking the water in Ephesus causes you to have stomach ailments,[e] drink some wine instead.]

[24]There are some who seek ordination, but their sins stand out and are well known. Yet there are others whose sins are not as obvious, but the truth of who they really are will eventually be seen and will bring them judgment.[f] [25]It is the same way with good works, even if they are not known at first, they will eventually be recognized and acknowledged.

---

a 5:18 See Deuteronomy 25:4.
b 5:18 Leviticus 19:13; Deuteronomy 24:15.
c 5:20 Or "fear." That is, the congregation will see proper correction and fear falling into sin.
d 5:21 This word can refer to angels or men.
e 5:23 The Greek text literally means "bladder frequency." The translator has chosen to bracket this parenthetical verse to show it is inserted in the middle of Paul's words regarding the topic of ordination (laying on of hands). Paul does not encourage the drinking of wine, nor does he condemn its moderate use.
f 5:24 An alternate Aramaic translation is "there are some who confess their sins and bring them to judgment, and there are those whose sins follow them."

Six

---

¹Instruct every employee[a] to respect and honor their employers,[b] for this attitude presents to them a clear testimony of God's truth and renown. Tell them to never provide them with a reason to discredit God's name because of their actions. ²Especially honor and respect employers who are believers and don't despise them, but serve them all the more, for they are fellow believers. They should be at peace with them as beloved members of God's family. Be faithful to teach them these things as their sacred obligation.

³But if anyone teaches other doctrines that are contrary to the truth, teaching others that holy awe of God[c] is not important, then they prove they know nothing at all! It's obvious they don't value or hold dear the healing words of our Lord Jesus Christ. ⁴They are covered with the clouds of conceit. They are loaded[d] with controversy, and they love to argue their opinions and split hairs. The fruit of their ministry is contention and competition, causing people to think evil toward others and even toward God.

⁵They add misery to many lives by corrupting their minds and cheating them of the truth. They equate the worship of God with

---

a 6:1 Or "those under the yoke of performance (servitude or slavery)." The Greek text clearly refers to slaves and masters, but the Aramaic is somewhat ambiguous and could still be referring to the topic of Chapter 5. "Those" would refer to the leadership of the church instead—pastors, deacons, and deaconesses.

b 6:1 Or "masters." Also in verse 2.

c 6:3 The Aramaic here and in verse 6 literally means "the doctrine of the fear of God." The fear of God is one of the seven spirits of God, the spirit of the fear of God (Isaiah 11:2–3). To teach there is no fear of God would be leading people away from the Holy Spirit. The fear of God is more than simply loving and respecting God. There are over 100 references in both the Old and New Testaments that speak of "the fear of God."

d 6:4 The Aramaic literally means "sick with controversy."

making great sums of money.[a] Distance yourself from them and their teachings!

⁶We are truly wealthy. We have a "profit" that is greater than theirs—our holy awe of God! To have merely our necessities is to have enough.

⁷Isn't it true that our hands were empty when we came into the world, and when we leave this world our hands will be empty again?

⁸Because of this, food and clothing is enough to make us content.

⁹But those who crave the wealth of this world slip into spiritual snares. They become trapped by the troubles that come through their foolish and harmful desires, driven by greed and drowning in their own sinful pleasures. And they take others down with them into their corruption and eventual destruction.

¹⁰Loving money[b] is the first step toward all kinds of trouble. Some people run after it so much that they have given up their faith and have turned from Christ—and they will live to regret it. Craving more money pushes them away from the faith into error, compounding misery[c] in their lives!

¹¹Timothy, you are God's man, so run from all these errors. Instead, chase after true holiness, justice, faithfulness, love, hope,[d] and tender humility. ¹²There is a battle raging, so fight with faith for the winner's prize! Lay your hands upon eternal life, for this is your calling—celebrating in faith before the multitude of witnesses![e]

¹³So now, I instruct you before the God of Resurrection Life[f] and

---

a   6:5 Or "to be godly is the way to get rich."
b   6:10 Or "insatiable greed for money."
c   6:10 As translated from the Aramaic. The word "misery" can also mean "demon."
d   6:11 Or "patience."
e   6:12 As translated from the Aramaic.
f   6:13 Or "the God who resurrects all."

before Jesus, the Anointed One, who demonstrated a beautiful testimony even before Pontius Pilate, [14]that you follow this commission faithfully with a clear conscience[a] and without blemish until the appearing of our Lord Jesus, the Messiah.

[15]Yes, God will make himself visible in his own divine timing,[b] for he is the exalted God, the only Powerful One, the King over every king, and the Lord of Power! [16]He alone is the Immortal God,[c] living in the unapproachable light of divine glory! No one has ever seen his fullness, nor can they, for all the glory and endless authority of the universe belongs to him, forever and ever. Amen!

[17]To all the rich of this world, I command you not to be wrapped in thoughts of pride over your prosperity, or rely on your wealth, for your riches are unreliable and nothing compared to the Living God. Trust instead in the one who has lavished upon us all good things, fulfilling our every need.[d]

[18]Remind the wealthy to be rich in good works of extravagant generosity, so that they can experience true enrichment by means of their giving. [19]This will provide a beautiful foundation for their lives and secure for them a great future, as they lay their hands upon the meaning of true life.

[20]So, my son Timothy,[e] don't forget all that has been deposited within you. Escape from the empty echoes of men[f] and the perversion

---

a 6:14 Or "without defilement."

b 6:15 By implication, the second coming of Jesus.

c 6:16 Or "Incorruptible God."

d 6:17 Or "pleasure."

e 6:20 Paul uses an endearing variation of Timothy's name; it could almost be read "Oh Timmy." The translation includes the words, *my son*, to make this explicit.

f 6:20 This is an Aramaic figure of speech that means literally "daughters of the voice [echoes] of vanity." The Greek text reads "profane and vain babblings."

of twisted reasoning.[a] 21For those who claim to possess this so-called knowledge have already wandered from the true faith.

May God's grace empower you always!

Love in Christ,

Paul

---

a 6:20 As translated from the Aramaic, which also means, "false doctrines." The Greek is "false (so-called) science."

2 Timothy

HEAVEN'S URGENCY

Translator's Introduction to 2 Timothy

AT A GLANCE

Author: The apostle Paul

Audience: Timothy, Paul's spiritual son in the faith

Date: AD 65–67

Type of Literature: A letter

Major Themes: False teachers, false doctrine, suffering, perseverance, and faithfulness.

Outline:
Letter Opening — 1:1–2
Thanksgiving for Timothy's Faith — 1:3–5
Encouragement to Timothy — 1:6–2:13
Instructions for Timothy — 2:14–4:8
Letter Closing — 4:9–22

ABOUT 2 TIMOTHY

This could be called the last will and testament of Paul the apostle. Filled with warnings of the troubles that were ahead, this letter speaks to our generation with an unusual urgency. The outward display of religion must not entice the passionate and hungry, turning them away from the truth of the gospel. Paul's heart burns as he looks to the end of his journey and knows that death is near. He stirs our conscience with his emotional letter.

The urgency of this letter is Paul's revelation of the last days. Mentioned here in 2 Timothy more than any other letter, Paul warns, instructs, and challenges all of us to live a life of purity as the days grow evil. He gives us six analogies of the last days' servant of the Lord. The believer is compared to a soldier (2:3), an athlete (2:5), a farmer (2:6), a minister (2:15), a vessel (2:21), and a servant (2:24).

I believe there are many verses that could be considered the most important themes of the book, but perhaps 4:7–8 would contain the summary theme of the letter:

> I have fought an excellent fight. I have finished my full course and I've kept my heart full of faith. There's a crown of righteousness waiting in heaven for me, and I know that my Lord will reward me on his day of righteous judgment. And this crown is not only waiting for me, but for all who love and long for his unveiling.

As you read 2 Timothy, try to picture Paul sitting in a prison cell. He misses his wonderful disciple, Timothy. Picture Timothy reading this letter with a longing deep within to hear these final words from his spiritual dad. Their love is deep, their commitment to the gospel is powerful, and their desire to see the world reached with the love of Christ is real.

PURPOSE

Writing from prison and awaiting execution, Paul seeks to impart his final words of wisdom to his spiritual son, Timothy. He carries some of the concerns over from his first letter, such as dealing with false teachers. In this letter, however, Paul weaves together the themes of suffering, perseverance, and vindication in relation to his own experience and Christ's. Paul gives Timothy this example to encourage him in his own ministry, and also his Christian life.

AUTHOR AND AUDIENCE

Written in AD 65 shortly before his martyrdom at the order of the Roman emperor Nero, Paul wants to make sure Timothy is instructed about serving the church as God's man. There is a spiritual inheritance found in 2 Timothy for every true minister of the gospel and for every lover of God.

Many have recognized this letter as the most personal and heartfelt of all of Paul's writings. He names twenty-three individuals—both friends and foes. He opens his heart and gives intimate details of his life, and he shares his desire to see Timothy advance in his calling.

Apparently, Timothy is still in Ephesus fulfilling the mandate Paul gave him in his first letter. Paul writes to his spiritual son knowing that death is near. He longed to see Timothy again and desired to make sure he was encouraged to finish his race to the end.

MAJOR THEMES

False teachers and doctrine. Apparently the same situation of unorthodox teaching Paul addressed in his first letter was still a problem. This time Paul calls these false teachers out by name: Hymenaeus and Philetus "are like gangrene," he says, who "have already spread their poison to many." He urges Timothy to unapologetically preach the Word of Truth and stay away from their foolish arguments.

Suffering and perseverance. From a Roman prison, waiting to be executed, Paul urges his gospel coworker to suffer as he has for the gospel. Paul calls Timothy into such living not only because of his own willingness to suffer but also because of Christ's own experience of death. He drives home this calling for courage by offering shameful examples of believers who've betrayed such a calling. Instead, Timothy—and us—are called to persevere through suffering like Paul, and like Christ, in order to receive their reward.

Faithfulness in life and ministry. As you might expect from a last will and testament, Paul instructs Timothy to pick up where he left off by carrying out his ministry with dedication and faithfully preaching the apostolic message. Paul offers his own life as an example of the kind of faithfulness to ministry and godliness he is urging Timothy to follow.

———

May your heart begin to burn with the Holy Spirit's fire as you read this letter of heavenly urgency. And may you be strengthened in grace to be faithful to finish your life's race with passion and love to the very end!

One

Dear Timothy,

[1]I am writing you as your apostolic father, appointed by God's pleasure to announce the wonderful promise of life found in Jesus, the anointed Messiah.

[2]My beloved son, I pray for a greater release of God's grace, love, and total well-being to flow into your life from God our Father and from our Lord Jesus Christ!

[3]You know that I've been called to serve the God of my fathers with a clean conscience. [4]Night and day I pray for you, thanking God for your life! I know that you have wept for me, your spiritual father, and your tears are dear to me. I can't wait to see you again! I'm filled with joy [5]as I think of your strong faith that was passed down through your family line. It began with your grandmother Lois, who passed it on to your dear mother, Eunice. And it's clear that you too are following in the footsteps of their godly example.

[6]I'm writing to encourage you to fan into a flame and rekindle[a] the fire of the spiritual gift God imparted to you when I laid my hands upon you.[b] [7]For God will never give you the spirit of fear,[c] but the Holy Spirit who gives you mighty power, love, and self-control.[d] [8]So never be ashamed of the testimony of our Lord, nor be embarrassed over my imprisonment, but overcome every evil by the revelation of the power

---

a   1:6 Literally "excite the gift" or "awake the gift."
b   1:6 Implied in the context.
c   1:7 That is, fearing men. The fear of God prevents us from fearing others.
d   1:7 The Aramaic can also be translated "revelation-light," or "instruction."

of God!^a ⁹He gave us resurrection life^b and drew us to himself by his holy calling on our lives. And it wasn't because of any good we have done, but by his divine pleasure and marvelous grace that confirmed our union with the anointed Jesus, even before time began!^c ¹⁰This truth is now being unveiled by the revelation of the anointed Jesus, our Life-Giver, who has dismantled death, obliterating all its effects on our lives, and has manifested his immortal life in us by the gospel.

¹¹And he has anointed^d me as his preacher, his apostle, and his teacher of truth to the nations. ¹²The confidence of my calling enables me to overcome every difficulty without shame, for I have an intimate revelation of this God. And my faith in him convinces me that he is more than able to keep all that I've placed in his hands safe and secure until the fullness of his appearing.

¹³Allow the healing words you've heard from me to live in you and make them a model for life as your faith and love for the Anointed One grows even more. ¹⁴Guard well this incomparable treasure by the Spirit of Holiness living within you.

¹⁵Perhaps you've heard that Phygelus,^e and Hermogenes^f and all the believers of Asia have deserted me because of my imprisonment. ¹⁶Nevertheless, so many times Onesiphorus^g was like a breath of fresh air to me and never seemed to be ashamed of my chains. May our Lord Jesus bestow compassion and mercy upon him and his household.

---

a   1:8 Or "with the gospel and the power of God."

b   1:9 Or "He is our Life-Giver."

c   1:9 Literally "before the time of the ages."

d   1:11 Or "consecrated."

e   1:15 His name means "fugitive."

f   1:15 His name means "born of Hermes," a pagan god.

g   1:16 His name means "one who brings profit" or "profitable" or "help-bringer." The Orthodox tradition recognizes Onesiphorus as one of the seventy disciples chosen and sent by Jesus to preach. He became a bishop at Colophon (Asia Minor) and later at Corinth. Both the Orthodox and Roman Catholic churches hold that he died a martyr outside of Ephesus in the city of Parium.

[17]For when he arrived in Rome, he searched and searched for me until he found out where I was being held, so that he could minister to me, [18]just like he did so wonderfully as I rested in his house[a] while in Ephesus, as you well know.

May Jesus, our Master, give him abundant mercy in the day he stands before him.

Two

[1]Timothy, my dear son,[b] live your life empowered by God's free-flowing grace, which is your true strength, found in the anointing of Jesus and your union with him! [2]And all that you've learned from me, confirmed by the integrity of my life,[c] pass on to faithful leaders who are competent to teach the congregations the same revelation.

[3]Overcome every form of evil[d] as a victorious soldier of Jesus the Anointed One. [4]For every soldier called to active duty must divorce himself from the distractions of this world so that he may fully satisfy the one who chose him.

[5]An athlete who doesn't play by the rules will never receive the trophy, so remain faithful to God![e]

---

a 1:18 This is an alternate translation of the Aramaic words found in verse 16. The translator has placed them here for the sake of the English narrative.

b 2:1 The Greek text literally means "my little child," and is used as a term of endearment.

c 2:2 Or "by way of many witnesses." These "witnesses" could be those people who also heard Paul's teaching, or it may refer to the prophetic confirmations of the truth he taught to Timothy.

d 2:3 As translated from the Aramaic. The Greek says "suffer hardships."

e 2:5 Supplied by the context to complete the ellipsis.

⁶The farmer who labors to produce a crop should be the first one to be fed from its harvest.

⁷Carefully consider all that I've taught you, and may our Lord inspire you with wisdom and revelation in everything you say and do. ⁸But make Jesus, the Anointed One, your focus in life and ministry. For he came to earth as the descendant of David and rose from the dead, according to the revelation of the gospel that God has given me. ⁹This is the reason I am persecuted and imprisoned by evildoers,ᵃ enduring the suffering of these chains—but the Word of God can never be chained! ¹⁰I endure all these hardships for the benefit of the chosen onesᵇ in Christ so that they may also discover the overcoming life that is in Jesus Christ, and experience a glory that lasts forever!

¹¹You can trust these words: If we were joined with him in his death, then we are joined with him in his life! ¹²If we are joined with him in his sufferings,ᶜ then we will reign together with him in his triumph. But if we disregard him, then he will also disregard us. ¹³But even if we are faithless, he will still be full of faith, for he never wavers in his faithfulness to us!ᵈ

¹⁴Be committed to teach the believers all these things when you are with them in the presence of the Lord. Instruct them to never be drawn into meaningless arguments, or tear each other down with useless words that only harm others.

---

a 2:9 The Greek text means "imprisoned as a criminal." However, the Aramaic word used here for "persecuted" can also be translated "crucified." Perhaps Paul is giving a prophecy of what would come. Later, Paul was indeed martyred either by crucifixion or beheading for his faith in Christ.

b 2:10 The Greek word here for "chosen" has embedded within it the word *logos*. God's chosen ones have been chosen by the Word of God to become a living word sent from his mouth to reveal the message of their destiny.

c 2:12 An alternate Aramaic translation could read "If we preach the kingdom, we shall rule with him."

d 2:13 Or "He will not be unfaithful to himself."

[15]Always be eager[a] to present yourself before God as a perfect and mature minister, without shame, as one who correctly explains the Word of Truth.

[16]And avoid empty chatter and worthless words,[b] for they simply add to the irreverence of those who converse in that manner. [17]For the words of Hymenaeus[c] and Philetus are like gangrene, they have already spread their poison to many. [18]They are lost to the truth and teach gross error when they teach that the resurrection of the dead has already passed.[d] They are guilty of subverting[e] the faith of some believers.

[19]But the firm[f] foundation of God has written upon it these two inscriptions: "The Lord God recognizes those who are truly his!"[g] and, "Everyone who worships the name of the Lord Jesus[h] must forsake wickedness!"[i]

[20]In a palace you find many kinds of containers and tableware for many different uses. Some are beautifully inlaid with gold or silver, but some are made of wood or earthenware; some of them are used for banquets and special occasions, and some for everyday use. [21]But you, Timothy, must not see your life and ministry this way. Your life and

---

a   2:15 An alternate Aramaic translation is "Don't become frustrated." The Greek word is *spoudazo*, an aorist imperative verb that could be translated, "Hurry and keep on hurrying," or "Consider it a serious matter and keep on considering it something serious to present yourself before God."

b   2:16 The Greek text could be translated "avoid corrupt and useless speakers," referring not to the words themselves, but to those who teach the flock. See verse 18.

c   2:17 See footnote for 1 Timothy 1:20.

d   2:18 Or in the Aramaic "never going to happen."

e   2:18 The Greek literally means "turning upside down the faith of some."

f   2:19 Or "true." An alternate Aramaic translation of this verse could read "that resurrection is the firm foundation," referring to verse 18.

g   2:19 See Numbers 16:5.

h   2:19 Or "Lord." By implication it is the Lord Jesus.

i   2:19 An alternate Aramaic translation could read "He will save from wickedness."

ministry must not be disgraced, for you are to be a pure container of Christ and dedicated to the honorable purposes of your Master, prepared[a] for every good work that he gives you to do.

²²Run as fast as you can from all the ambitions and lusts[b] of youth; and chase after all that is pure. Whatever builds up your faith and deepens your love must become your holy pursuit. And live in peace with all those who worship our Lord Jesus with pure hearts.

²³Stay away from all the foolish arguments of the immature, for these disputes will only generate more conflict. ²⁴For a true servant of our Lord Jesus will not be argumentative[c] but gentle toward all and skilled in helping others see the truth, having great patience toward the immature. ²⁵Then with meekness you'll be able to carefully enlighten those who argue with you so they can see God's gracious gift of repentance and be brought to the truth. ²⁶This will cause them to rediscover themselves[d] and escape from the snare of Satan who caught them in his trap so that they would carry out his purposes.

Three

¹But you need to be aware that in the final days the culture of society will become extremely fierce and difficult for the people of God.

---

a 2:21 Or in the Aramaic "appreciated."
b 2:22 The Greek text literally means "revolutionary desires."
c 2:24 An alternate Aramaic translation could read "you should not be argumentative with a true servant of the Lord."
d 2:26 Or "come to their senses."

²People will be self-centered lovers of themselves[a] and obsessed with money. They will boast of great things as they strut around in their arrogant pride and mock all that is right. They will ignore their own families.[b] They will be ungrateful[c] and ungodly.

³They will become addicted to hateful and malicious slander.[d] Slaves to their desires, they will be ferocious, belligerent haters of what is good and right. ⁴With brutal treachery, they will act without restraint, bigoted and wrapped in clouds of their conceit. They will find their delight in the pleasures of this world more than the pleasures of the loving God.

⁵They may pretend to have a respect for God, but in reality they want nothing to do with God's power. Stay away from people like these! ⁶For they are the ones who worm their way into the hearts of vulnerable women,[e] spending the night with those who are captured by their lusts and steeped in sin. ⁷They are always learning and wanting to teach,[f] but never discover the revelation-knowledge of truth.

⁸History has given us an example of this with the Egyptian sorcerers Jannes and Jambres,[g] who stood against Moses in their arrogance.

---

a 3:2 Or in the Aramaic "men will look out only for themselves."

b 3:2 Or "disloyal to their people." The Greek is "disobedient to parents."

c 3:2 The Aramaic literally means "rejecters of grace."

d 3:3 Because this phrase is also the description of the Devil (the accuser or slanderer), it could be translated "they will be devils."

e 3:6 An alternate Greek translation could read "they intrude into households and by their heresies, take prisoners of those who are led astray by desires and sins." The Aramaic, however, is clearly speaking of the gross immorality of the last days.

f 3:7 Implied in the Aramaic.

g 3:8 This is a fascinating verse, for Jannes and Jambres are never mentioned by name in Exodus. It simply mentions the sorcerers who wanted to compete with Moses and his authority. These two names are, however, mentioned by Origen, one of the church fathers, who makes reference to the Book of Jannes and Jambres, but no complete copies of these books have ever been found.

So it will be in the last days with those who reject the faith with their corrupt minds and arrogant hearts, standing against the truth of God.

⁹But they will not advance, for everyone will see their madness, just as they did with Jannes and Jambres![a]

¹⁰But you, Timothy, have closely followed my example and the truth that I've imparted to you. You have modeled your life after the love and endurance I've demonstrated in my ministry by not giving up. The faith I have, you now have. What I have hungered for in life has now become your longing as well. The patience I have with others, you now demonstrate. ¹¹And the same persecutions and difficulties I have endured, you have also endured. Yes, you know all about what I had to suffer while in Antioch, Iconium, and Lystra. You're aware of all the persecution I endured there; yet the Lord delivered me from every single one of them! ¹²For all who choose to live passionately and faithfully as worshipers of Jesus, the Anointed One, will also experience persecution.

¹³But the evil men and sorcerers[b] will progress from bad to worse, deceived and deceiving, as they lead people further from the truth. ¹⁴Yet you must continue to advance in strength with the truth wrapped around your heart, being assured by God that he's the One[c] who has truly taught you all these things.

¹⁵Remember what you were taught from your childhood from the Holy Scrolls[d] which can impart to you wisdom to experience everlasting life through the faith of Jesus, the Anointed One! ¹⁶Every Scripture[e] has

---

a   3:9 Implied in the conclusion of Paul's argument.
b   3:13 Or "deceivers." The Greek word is "sorcerers."
c   3:14 By implication "God." However, some interpret this as his teachers.
d   3:15 Or "sacred Scriptures."
e   3:16 Keep in mind that when Paul wrote this he was referring to the Torah and all the Old Testament writings. Today, "every Scripture" would include the New Testament as well.

been written by the Holy Spirit, the breath of God. It will empower you by its instruction and correction, giving you the strength to take the right direction and lead you deeper into the path of godliness. [17]Then you will be God's servant, fully mature and perfectly prepared to fulfill any assignment God gives you.

Four

——

[1]Timothy, in the presence[a] of our great God and our Lord Jesus Christ, the One who is destined to judge both the living and the dead by the revelation of his kingdom—I solemnly instruct you to [2]proclaim the Word of God and stand upon it no matter what! Rise to the occasion and preach when it is convenient and when it is not. Preach in the full expression of the Holy Spirit[b]—with wisdom and patience as you instruct and teach the people.

[3]For the time is coming when they will no longer listen and respond to the healing words of truth because they will become selfish and proud. They will seek out teachers with soothing words that line up with their desires, saying just what they want to hear. [4]They will close their ears to the truth and believe nothing but fables and myths.[c] So be alert to all these things and overcome every form of evil. [5]Carry in your

---

a 4:1 Or "before the eyes of God." The Greek word is *enopion*, which could be translated "within eyesight of." Imagine looking into heaven and seeing the eyes of God gazing at you. This is the strength of Paul's charge to Timothy.

b 4:2 As translated from the Aramaic.

c 4:4 Or in the Aramaic "ritualistic ceremonies."

heart the passion of your calling as a church planter[a] and evangelist, and fulfill your ministry calling.[b]

[6]And now the time is fast approaching for my release from this life and I am ready to be offered as a sacrifice.[c] [7]I have fought an excellent fight. I have finished my full course and I've kept my heart full of faith. [8]There's a crown of righteousness waiting in heaven for me, and I know that my Lord will reward me on his day of righteous judgment. And this crown is not only waiting for me, but for all who love and long for his unveiling.[d]

[9]Please come as soon as you can [10]since Demas deserted me and has left to go to Thessalonica, for he loves his own life.[e] Crescens has gone to Galatia, and Titus has gone to Dalmatia. [11]That leaves only Luke with me, so find Mark and bring him with you, for he is a tremendous help for me in my ministry.

[12]I have also dispatched Tychicus to Ephesus to minister there. [13]When you come, please bring the leather book bag[f] along with the books I left in Troas with Carpus—especially the parchment scrolls.

[14]You need to know that Alexander,[g] the jeweler,[h] has done me

---

a 4:5 Implied in the concept of being a New Testament evangelist. Apostolic missionaries sent out to evangelize were to plant churches wherever they ministered. Our contemporary concept of an evangelist is quite different than in Paul's day.

b 4:5 Or "being confident in your ministry."

c 4:6 Or "poured out as a drink offering."

d 4:8 Or "sudden appearance."

e 4:10 Or "he loves the world."

f 4:13 The Aramaic literally means "carrying case." This would have been a bag made of leather or woolen cloth. The Greek text reads "bring the cloak." The Aramaic words for "book" and "cloak" are nearly identical, which would explain the Greek mistranslation using "cloak." It is fascinating that the aged Paul, nearing death, found his heart attached to the manuscripts and books that undoubtedly expounded on the Old Testament writings. He knew Jesus intimately, yet longed for more revelation of the written Word until his death.

g 4:14 Alexander means "protector of men" or "man-pleaser."

h 4:14 The word used here can also be "silversmith," "blacksmith" or "coppersmith."

great harm. May our Lord give him what he deserves for all he has done. ¹⁵Be careful of him, for he arrogantly opposes our ministry.

¹⁶At first there was no one I could count on to faithfully stand with me—they all ran off and abandoned me—but don't hold this against them. ¹⁷For in spite of this, my Lord himself stood with me, empowering me to complete my ministry of preaching to all the non-Jewish nations so they all could hear the message and be delivered from the mouth of the lion![a] ¹⁸And my Lord will continue to deliver me from every form of evil and give me life in his heavenly kingdom. May all the glory go to him alone for all the ages of eternity!

¹⁹Please give my warm regards[b] to Prisca and to Aquila[c] and to Onesiphorus and his family.

²⁰Erastus has remained in Corinth, but Trophimus I had to leave in Miletus due to his illness.[d]

²¹Do your best to come before winter.

Eubulus sends his greetings, along with Pudens, Linus,[e] and Claudia, and all those in prison with me.

²²May the anointing of our Lord Jesus be with your spirit and his grace overflow to you!

Love in Christ,
Paul

---

a 4:17 Or "that they will hear that I have been delivered from the mouth of the lion." By implication, the lion is a metaphor for the Devil.

b 4:19 The Aramaic literally means "give peace."

c 4:19 Prisca is a diminutive form of Priscilla ("long life"). She and her husband, Aquila ("eagle"), were tentmakers like Paul. They were not only business partners with Paul, but also partners with him in ministry. See Acts 18:2, 18, and 26; Rom. 16:3; and 1 Cor. 16:19.

d 4:20 The Greek word used here can refer to physical or spiritual ailments.

e 4:21 In church history it was widely accepted and stated by Irenaeus that Linus was a disciple of Peter and became the bishop of Rome.

About The Passion Translation

The message of God's story is timeless; the Word of God doesn't change. But the methods by which that story is communicated should be timely; the vessels that steward God's Word can and should change.

One of those timely methods and vessels is Bible translations. Bible translations are both a gift and a problem. They give us the words God spoke through his servants, but words can become very poor containers for revelation— they leak! Over time the words change from one generation to the next.

Meaning is influenced by culture, background, and many other details. There is no such thing as a truly literal translation of the Bible, for there is not an equivalent language that perfectly conveys the meaning of the biblical text except as it is understood in its original cultural and linguistic setting. Therefore, a translation can be a problem. The problem, however, is solved when we seek to transfer meaning, and not merely words, from the original text to the receptor language.

The Passion Translation is a new, heart-level translation that expresses God's fiery heart of love to this generation using Hebrew, Greek, and Aramaic manuscripts, merging the emotion and life-changing truth of God's Word.

God longs to have his Word expressed in every language in a way that unlocks the passion of his heart. The goal of this work is to trigger inside every reader an overwhelming response to the truth of the Bible, unfolding the deep mysteries of the Scriptures in the love language of God, the language of the heart.

We pray and trust this version of God's Word will kindle in you a burning, passionate desire for him and his heart, while impacting the church for years to come!

About the Translator

Dr. Brian Simmons is known as a passionate lover of God. After a dramatic conversion to Christ, Brian knew that God was calling him to go to the unreached people of the world and present the gospel of God's grace to all who would listen. With his wife Candice and their three children, he spent nearly eight years in the tropical rain forest of the Darien Province of Panama as a church planter, translator, and consultant. Brian was involved in the Paya-Kuna New Testament translation project. He studied linguistics and Bible translation principles with New Tribes Mission. After their ministry in the jungle, Brian was instrumental in planting a thriving church in New England (U.S.), and now travels full time as a speaker and Bible teacher. He has been happily married to Candice for over forty-two years and is known to boast regularly of his children and grandchildren. Brian and Candice may be contacted at:

Facebook.com/passiontranslation
Twitter.com/tPtBible

For more information about the translation project or any of Brian's books, please visit:

thepassiontranslation.com
stairwayministries.org

thePassionTranslation.com